COASTAL HOMEOWNERS

THE COMPLETE PHOTO GUIDE TO COASTAL
MAINTENANCE

ADAPT YOUR HOME TO THE COASTAL
ENVIRONMENT

D1568716

Copyright © 2011
All rights reserved
ISBN 978-0-615-51393-5
Printed in USA
www.coastalhomebook.com

Contents

Coastal Homeowners

The Complete Photo Guide To Coastal Maintenance

Contents

The Complete Photo Guide To Coastal Maintenance

Adapt Your Home To The Coastal Environment

ACKNOWLEDGMENTS

I want to thank my wife, Elizabeth, a licensed general contractor, for her assistance, continued support, and patience while I developed this book. Thanks to Sun-Surf Realty, Braswell Carpet Cleaning, and Kellum Heating and Air for their professional services and for allowing me to photograph work in progress. I would like to thank coastal carpenter Chris Gray for his knowledge of the coastal environment and for lending a helping hand. Thanks also to photo editor Ron Howard, editor Roxanne Raynor, and graphic designer, James Clark for their expertise and assistance.

The following companies contributed photographs to this project: PGT Industries doors and windows, Weather Shield MFG doors and windows, Jamsill Guard sill pans, Pactiv Building Products building wrap, Versatex trimboards, CertainTeed siding and trim, Plycem USA trim products, Amana heating and air conditioning, Rheem water heaters, Metals USA roofing, Alutech United hurricane shutters, and Kohler Company residential generators.

NOTICE TO READERS

ABOUT THE BOOK

This photo guidebook was published to show coastal homeowners how to adapt their homes to the everyday challenges presented by a coastal environment. Salt air, salt spray, humidity, corrosion, wind-driven rain, nor'easters, tropical storms, and hurricanes are challenges that do not exist in inland regions. This book does not represent just another do-it-yourself book, although many of the everyday challenges can be tackled with relative ease. Instead, this book is a unique how-to book, helping homeowners eliminate trial and error and do it right the first time, while living in a coastal environment.

Best of all, most of the photos in this book were taken on location in coastal areas. As you will see, the coastal environment can easily deteriorate building materials not suitable for coastal elements. Materials and construction practices not designed for those elements will cost you thousands of dollars in repairs and repeat maintenance and will decrease home values. There are also photos showing solutions using products and construction practices that will give you years of worry-free maintenance.

The Complete Photo Guide To Coastal Maintenance is divided into thirteen chapters that deal with all aspects of protecting and maintaining the exterior and interior of your home from the coastal elements: including hardware, fasteners, and nails, doors and windows, exterior siding, coastal roofs, lighting and electrical components, heating and cooling, coastal decks, water heaters, exterior surface preparation, and preventative maintenance. There are also chapters addressing concerns about hurricane preparedness and winterizing coastal homes. We place emphasis on protecting your family and your coastal home by illustrating tips, techniques, and solutions and making them practical and accessible to coastal homeowners.

The final chapter, "Increasing Rental Income," is essential reading for those coastal homeowners who are considering or have already purchased or built a home for investment purposes. Millions of vacationers travel to the coastal areas annually and book rental properties. The expectation of today's guests is very high. The photos and information in this chapter will give you tips and solutions that have been proven to increase rental income.

The Coastal Products Directory, located in the Appendix, is a comprehensive and valuable reference guide with more than one hundred companies, marketing many of their products to the coastal homeowner. Their products are resistant to salt air, salt spray, humidity, corrosion, wind-driven rain, and hurricanes.

The next time you meet with a contractor or handyman about your next home improvement project or a maintenance issue, the photos and information gathered in this book will help you choose the best low-maintenance products and construction practices and will eliminate many repairs and repeat maintenance problems.

The Complete Photo Guide To Coastal Maintenance is a book with more than three hundred full-color photographs that we hope you will find to be practical and useful while living near the beautiful seashores and coastal sounds of this country.

ABOUT THE AUTHOR

Wayne Higson is a quality-control manager. He has been a licensed general contractor in North Carolina since 1989. Living in North Carolina, Higson would often vacation at the beach, enjoying the sand, surf, and warm salty breeze. He would often see trawlers trying to catch their bounty of shrimp; it is a wonderful attraction.

In 1993, he built a vacation home on the Crystal Coast of North Carolina. At that time, he was unaware of how quickly the coastal environment could damage, deteriorate, and corrode most materials used in the "average" building process. In particular, windows, doors, hardware exterior siding, light fixtures, paint, heating and cooling systems, and roofing were vulnerable to the coastal environment.

Through painstaking research, along with trial and error, Higson was able to find solutions, along with products, that could reduce his maintenance and repair costs. The information and products he found also minimized repeat maintenance costs or eliminated them altogether. As a result, he saved time and money and was able to increase his property value and rental income.

Of course, it would have been a great benefit for him to have had this information when he began his construction—which is why he decided to write this unique, easy-to-follow photo guidebook for you. Too often, Higson sees coastal homeowners spending excessive amounts of time on expensive repairs and repeat maintenance, just as he did. He is dedicated to making sure that all coastal homeowners benefit from the lessons he has learned.

PREFACE

A Dream Gone Wrong

Mark and Patti dreamed of having a house by the sea. For years, they worked hard as they raised their small family, nurturing the goals and achievements of their four children. Then, with their children either on their own or comfortably finishing up college, they realized the time had finally arrived for them to turn their attention to *their* dream—the coastal home they'd always wanted.

They knew exactly where they wanted to live and bought a cottage in the beach community where they'd vacationed when the children were small. Just a block from the beach, the house was close enough to smell the ocean.

"We loved the community," Patti said. "We'd rented a number of houses over the years in different areas and on different streets. We knew exactly where we wanted our house to be."

"As soon as we saw a house come on the market, we put in a bid," Mark added.

"The house needed some work before we moved in," Patti said. "We wanted to install new hardware and light fixtures and add a couple of bedrooms so that the kids could visit whenever they wanted."

The kitchen and bathroom needed to be modernized. Mark was pleased that the new second floor would allow for an ocean view, something that would not only add value to the property but also be a real asset to their enjoyment of the house.

"We aren't rich but we had saved our money just to be able to do this," Mark said, "so we weren't pinching pennies. We wanted the best, but we did not consider what the coastal environment would do to our beautiful new remodel."

When the construction was finished, and the landscaper did his magic on their small yard, the house was "perfect."

"It was exactly what we wanted," Patti exclaimed, "pretty as a postcard."

They would have been better off with the postcard. The first summer was everything they'd hoped for, but by the time the next summer came around, rust was already corroding the hinges on the garden gate, and streaks of rust marred the side of the house. The wood floor was buckling in one of the back bedrooms. The kick plate on the front door and the exterior light fixtures were tarnished and pitted. The doorknobs looked like they were a hundred years old. The roof was in need of repair.

"It was a nightmare," Mark conceded with a shudder. "The house had become an eyesore. It wasn't just how things were looking, either; it was worse than that. Things didn't work. The air-conditioner guy said that the unit could be repaired but recommended replacement." Mark and Patti's dream house had truly become a nightmare.

Things didn't have to turn out the way they did. If Patti and Mark had simply understood the coastal environment and followed the insights I will share with you in this book, their picture-postcard perfect house would have stayed that way for many years.

Whether your dream house is for yourself, a rental, or an investment, you owe it to yourself to make sure that it does not become a nightmare.

By the sea, by the sea, by the beautiful sea ...we will play by the sea, by the beautiful sea ...

INTRODUCTION~THE COASTAL ENVIRONMENT

I t seems that everyone wants to live at the beach, or close to it. The narrow fringes of land that define our coastal areas are a wealth of natural and economic resources and are among the most developed parcels of land in the nation. Making up just 17 percent of our nation's land, the coasts are home to more than half of the nation's population. There is no question; everyone wants to live at the beach!

From 1980 to 2003, the population of our coastal areas grew by 33 million people. 23 of the 25 most densely populated counties in the United States were coastal counties. What's more, the growth and development of these coastal areas is only increasing.

There's nothing wrong with that. We all want to be close to the sand and the sea. However, if we want to enjoy our homes in this beautiful environment, we had better

The Crystal Coast, Emerald Isle, NC. Photo courtesy of Frank Rush, Town Manager.

respect that living on the coast is not like living anyplace else; there are environmental challenges that don't exist in inland communities. Unless you understand and factor in these environmental challenges when buying, building, or maintaining your coastal home, it can cost you thousands of dollars in repairs, replacement costs, and property values. You will find yourself like Mark and Patti, bemoaning a dream house that has become a nightmare.

The ocean is a wonderful attraction. The sand and surf are compelling reasons to live close to the shore, but the salty environment causes significant corrosion and pitting—destroying metals and other materials that would remain pristine in a different environment. Wind-driven rains, tropical storms, hurricanes, nor'easters—the coast has weather patterns and environmental conditions that prove to be a challenge to coastal homeowners who want to keep their homes looking and functioning as they should.

A challenge, yes, but one that you can accomplish. Smart planning, smart choices, and attention to detail will prove invaluable in adapting your home to the coastal environment.

In the following chapters, we will explore the best choices in construction methods and low-maintenance products, which will save you time and money—not to mention many, many headaches!

1

Hardware, Fasteners, and Nails

*T*he brass-plated entrance hardware on this expensive fiber-glass door has already corroded. The salt-air will quickly tarnish and corrode hardware not designed for the coastal environment.

Coastal homeowners should always consider the salt-air environment when choosing exterior hardware, fasteners, and nails.

This chapter will show how an uninformed decision in this area can easily lead to more maintenance, cost, and frustration. It will introduce you to hardware, fasteners, and nails that are corrosion-resistant and low maintenance and will last for years in a salt-air environment. Products that offer a better value and are available at your coastal hardware or home improvement store.

This Chapter Includes
Door Knobs And Deadbolts (entry hardware)
Exterior Hinges and Latches
Interior Hinges
Screws and Nails

In a perfect world, once fasteners and hardware were installed, you would never have to think about them again. Hinges would work flawlessly, allowing entry doors to swing open easily, without a squeak. Unfortunately, the coastal world, while beautiful and inviting, is not perfect. As a result, hardware that looks beautiful on store shelves will quickly look dated and pitted with use. Patti learned the hard way that things hidden only stay hidden and out of the way as long as they continue to work!

Doorknobs and Deadbolts (entry hardware)

Just as eyes are the windows to the soul, your front door speaks volumes about your coastal home. You want it to be warm and inviting. I will explain about the door itself later; for now, let's look at what your doorknob says about your home—and I'm not talking about the style here. The brass-plated doorknob and deadbolt in the photos below have already corroded in the coastal environment, while stainless steel hardware continues to look new for years.

Which house is more inviting? The one with the clean, solid look! While stainless steel entry hardware is corrosion resistant, unlike brass it is very limited in style and design for residential homes. Homeowners will often decide on style and finish before considering material construction. A coastal homeowner will quickly realize material construction and durability of finish are more important. Replacing corroded entry hardware can be expensive. First lesson learned...

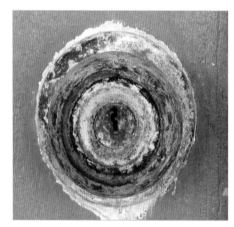

The brass-plated deadbolt and doorknob have already corroded. The key cylinders will be hard, or impossible, to turn with a key.

However, the stainless steel deadbolt and doorknob are corrosion-resistant and will work flawlessly for years.

Have you ever noticed that some metal-plated entry hardware will have a lifetime finish warranty that does not exclude the salt-air environment, even on oceanfront or soundside homes? The salt-air will tarnish and corrode the product, and the manufacturer will still replace it at no cost. All you have to do is spend the time, labor, and money to remove, return and reinstall the same type of entry hardware that will only corrode again. Replacing metal-plated entry hardware, even with a lifetime finish warranty, can be frustrating and expensive for the coastal homeowner.

When choosing brass, always opt for solid brass—coated many times with a durable finish. Ask about lifetime-finish warranties, and make sure they do not exclude the salt-air environment—specifically, oceanfront, oceanside, or soundside properties. A bright solid brass finish may require waxing and polishing.

The same salt-air, sand, and grit that caused the hardware to tarnish, pit, and corrode can make it nearly impossible to unlock your door. When installing a doorknob (lockset) and deadbolt, always orient the key-hole

cylinder so that the internal pins are at the top. If necessary, a locksmith or hardware specialist at your local home improvement store can rotate the internal cylinder pins for you. As the photo shows, when inserting your key in the cylinder, the key cuts (notches) in the key should orient up. Sand, grit, and salt-moisture will settle in the bottom of the key cylinder. By rotating the internal cylinder pins up, you will keep salt-moisture, sand, and grit from settling on the pins, ensuring a longer, smoother lock life. A lesson learned from a coastal locksmith.

Speaking of cylinder pins, whether your lockset is stainless steel or solid brass, lubricate it annually, or you may find that your key will not turn the cylinder, leaving you locked out and having to call a locksmith. Another lesson learned...

Solid brass entry lockset with polished brass finish. Other solid brass finishes may include satin brass, antique and satin nickel, satin black, or polished and satin chrome.

13

Exterior Hinges and Latches

Nothing distracts from the look of a door or gate, or diminishes how comfortably it operates, than a rusted, corroded hinge or latch. Always opt for stainless steel hinges and latches. The greater initial cost will pay for itself many times over as the months and years pass. And, make sure that you use stainless steel screws! Never compromise a good hinge by scrimping on the screws. Stainless steel hinges and latches can be purchased at a coastal hardware or home improvement store.

Metal-plated gate hinges will corrode in a salt-air environment.

Corrosion-resistant stainless steel gate hinge with stainless steel screws.

Galvanized gate latch and screws will corrode in a salt-air environment.

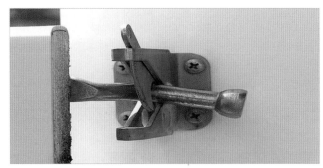

Stainless steel gate latch with stainless steel screws.

Corroded metal-plated exterior door hinge.

Stainless steel exterior door hinge with stainless steel screws.

Interior Hinges

Most interior door units are purchased with metal-plated hinges. The interior of your home is often exposed to the outside environment. When windows and doors are open, the salt-air will enter your home, slowly deteriorating your interior hardware. It can be expensive to install stainless steel or solid brass hinges on all your interior doors. A less expensive alternative is to apply a clear lacquer coating to both sides of the door hinge to increase corrosion protection. This practice will help a metal-plated door hinge maintain the factory appearance much longer.

Tarnished and corroded interior brass-plated hinge without a lacquer coating.

Clear lacquer being applied to an interior brass-plated hinge to protect the finish from tarnishing in the salt-air environment, for longer-lasting beauty.

Screws and Nails

Have you ever walked past a beautifully constructed beach home only to see, upon closer inspection, that it has been "crying" brown tears? That's right, streaks of brown are staining its exterior. Those streaks are nothing but the rust from a poorly chosen nail or wood screw.

Hot-dipped galvanized and zinc-plated siding nails will corrode in a salt-air environment. Use stainless steel siding nails on your coastal home, particularly ocean-front, oceanside, or soundside homes. A lesson learned…

We have said it before and we will say it again: Never scrimp on screws or nails. Use materials that are resistant to corrosion.

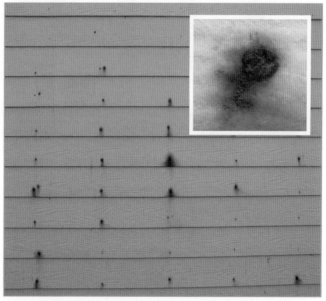

Corroded nail heads on exterior siding. The method of repair will be addressed in a later chapter.

304 Stainless Steel Screws

18/8 Stainless Steel (18% Chrome— 8% Nickel) Also called 304 stainless.

Excellent anti-corrosion properties. 18/8 stainless steel is non-magnetic ideal in the coastal environment.

316 Stainless Steel Screws

These are more corrosion resistant than 18/8 stainless steel. They are non-magnetic containing approximately 12% nickel and a minimum of 16% chromium; they also contain approximately 2.5% molybdenum (moly). With the increased nickel and added moly, this alloy composition is better suited to high-chloride environments, such as oceanfront, oceanside, or soundside properties. There is no visual difference between 304 and 316 stainless steel. **Note:** *Most coastal hardware or home improvement stores supply the higher grade screws made of 316 stainless steel.*

316 Stainless Steel Sheet-Metal Screw.

Zinc-and Chrome-Plated Steel Screws

These screws are magnetic and made from low-strength steel. Like brass, it is softer than stainless steel. They are plated with zinc to improve rust resistance or chromed for a shiny decorative appearance. Never install zinc-or chrome-plated screws in a salt-air environment. A lesson Learned...

Salt air corroded and deteriorated each of these zinc-plated screws. Removing screws like these without damaging the adjoining surface can be a challenge. These screws were replaced with type 316 stainless steel screws.

Solid Brass Screws

Unlike stainless steel, which can have some magnetic properties, especially the lower-grade stainless steels, (refer to chapter thirteen pg.140) solid brass screws are non-magnetic, they will not corrode or bleed rust. Brass screws are not as strong as stainless steel screws and the finished surface will tarnish, losing it's shinny decorative appearance quickly in a salt-air environment.

Brass wood screw

Measuring Screws

The five most common head shapes include: flat head, oval head, round head, pan head, and hex head. When shopping for screws at your local coastal hardware or home improvement store, it is important to understand how each is measured to determine proper length.

Flat Head: measure from top of head to tip of screw.
Oval Head: measure from top of head to tip of screw.
Round Head: measure from under the head to tip of screw.
Pan Head: measure from under the head to tip of screw.
Hex Head: measure from under the head to tip of screw.

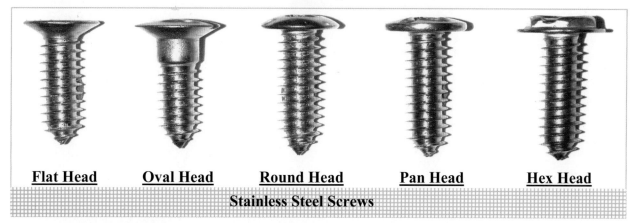

Flat Head   **Oval Head**   **Round Head**   **Pan Head**   **Hex Head**
Stainless Steel Screws

Carriage Screws

Unlike wood screws, which are threaded for at least 2/3 of their length and have a smooth neck between the thread and the head, or sheet-metal screws, which are threaded for their full length, carriage screws (also referred to as carriage bolts) have a dome shaped head and square neck that keep them from turning once they have been tightened. They are considered

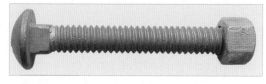

through bolts, used to fasten wood to wood or wood to metal. Hot-dipped galvanized or double hot-dipped galvanized carriage bolts are a good choice. **Note:** *A carriage bolt can only be tightened from the hex nut end. The drill hole for a carriage bolt will need to be precise. If not the square neck will turn inside the drilled hole, preventing the bolt from tightening. Because of this, some coastal building codes may restrict the use of carriage bolts used on a deck assembly.*

Lag Screws

These hex head screws are larger and longer than regular wood screws and have greater gripping power. Hot-dipped or double hot-dipped galvanized lag screws (often referred to as lag bolts) has the same resistance to corrosion as carriage bolts. **Note:** *Unlike the carriage bolt, lag bolts are not considered a through bolt. Through bolts will pass completely through the members being connected with a nut that tightens on the other side. To ensure structural integrity of a deck assembly, coastal building codes will prohibit the use of lag bolts. Deck fasteners and hardware are addressed in chapter six.*

When choosing fasteners, pay close attention to what is being fastened. What hardness does the job require? What length? Pay particular attention to the materials that will afford you the greatest rust and corrosion protection. Removing corroded screws can be almost impossible without causing damage to the surrounding area. It can be challenging even to change a light bulb in an exterior light fixture. A lesson learned.....

If the screws are corroded, you can easily damage a fixture when trying to change a light bulb. Check all your exterior fixtures for plated screws and replaced with stainless steel or solid brass screws.

Nails

The two most common nails for exterior applications in a coastal salt-air environment are hot-dipped galvanized and stainless steel. Zinc or galvanized-plated nails should not be considered.

Hot-Dipped Galvanized Nails

Hot-dipped galvanizing is a process of coating steel nails in molten zinc. Melting zinc is acknowledged by most authorities as the best way to apply a heavy uniform coating to a nail. Hot-dipped galvanized nails are corrosion resistant and used primarily for docks, decks, piers, and coastal homes. As the photo below shows, it is not the best choice for oceanfront, oceanside, or soundside homes when applying exterior siding and trim boards. Sea spray, salt-air, high winds, and wind-driven sand can weather the surface of the nail heads, removing the galvanized coating. Rust may soon appear on the nail heads and could compromise the long-term integrity of the siding. A lesson learned... We will address nail-head repair in a later chapter.

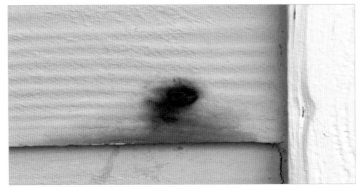

A close up view of a corroded hot-dipped galvanized nail head that has bled rust onto the siding. This results from not making the best choice when choosing a siding nail. Always opt for type 316 stainless steel siding nails; they will not corrode and bleed rust.

Stainless Steel Nails

Stainless steel nails are available in both 304 and 316 grades. These nails are great for all types of siding, trim, fiber-cement boards, and decks. Stainless steel nails are more corrosion resistant than hot-dipped galvanized nails. They are available in smooth finish, spiral, and ring shank styles at your coastal hardware or home improvement store. Stainless steel nails are a good choice for fastening treated lumber.

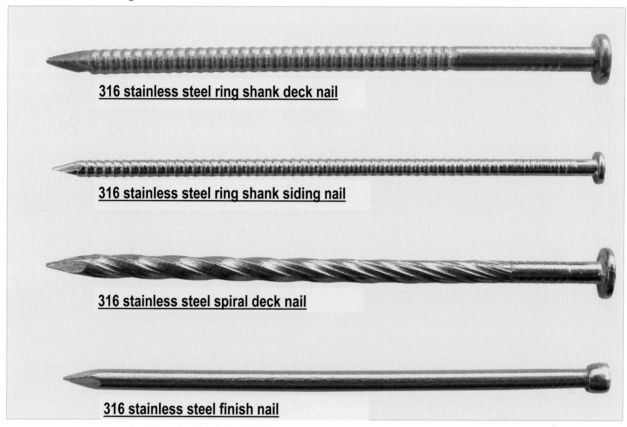

316 stainless steel ring shank deck nail

316 stainless steel ring shank siding nail

316 stainless steel spiral deck nail

316 stainless steel finish nail

When it comes to the "little things" like screws, nails, and hinges (the "hidden hardware"), never assume the contractor will choose the most corrosive-resistant finish or material. Never scrimp or pinch pennies when choosing nails. Make the right choice, and you will enjoy years of virtually maintenance-free beauty and function.

2

Doors and Windows

Doors and windows should be designed for the coastal environment. The photo shows a beautiful fiberglass entry-door system with glass sidelights and a solid-brass entry lock.

As a coastal homeowner, there are very few decisions more important than doors and windows. The investment can be substantial. Uninformed choices in this area will cost thousands of dollars in repairs, repeat maintenance and home values.

There is more to consider than style, energy efficiency, security, and view. A coastal homeowner will have to consider wind-driven rain, coastal storms, humidity, salt-air, and windblown debris. High winds caused by a nor'easter, tropical storm, hurricane, or a severe coastal storm will often force water upward in and around door and window seals, not designed for the coastal environment. This causes major water damage over time to walls and flooring, including wood rot.

This chapter will provide valuable information relating to door and window requirements, installation, care, and maintenance in coastal areas. Doors and windows that are high-impact resistant require minimum maintenance and will not corrode, rot, or swell.

This Chapter Includes
Entry Doors-Sliding Patio
Entry Doors-Hinged
Garage Doors
Windows
Moisture Management
Impact Zone (IZ)
Energy Performance Label

A Turkish proverb says, "A small key opens big doors." The truth is, if you don't have the right door, it will take more than a key to get it open. Doors and windows bring light and air into your home, or keep them out! Your doors allow you and your friends to enter and exit. Entryways often tell the story of a house. A clean, neat, welcoming entryway is inviting. One that is warped, corroded, cracked, and split is not.

Fiberglass entrance door with stainless steel hinges and entry lock.

Corroded galvanized-steel door not designed for the coastal environment.

Not only do you want your doors and windows to look good, you want and need them to work well. With wind-driven rain and the coastal environment, it is important to choose your doors and windows well and to perform simple, regular maintenance in order to avoid lengthy and costly repairs. Do your research; not all entry doors are designed for coastal conditions, high winds, wind-driven rain, and the corrosive environment. Door and window manufacturers may offer a coastal product line. These products may be assembled with stainless steel hardware, specially designed full-perimeter door and window seals, and high-impact glass. Doors and windows designed to withstand the coastal environment may be found in the Coastal Products Directory in the appendix section of this book.

Interior view of vinyl-clad sliding patio door.

Exterior view of vinyl-clad sliding patio door.

Entry Doors—Sliding Patio Doors

Sliding patio doors bring a great deal of air and light into a room. They provide a ready elegance and openness to the space. What's more, they do it without requiring room for a door to swing inward or outward.

Stay away from sliding doors that have not been designed or tested for coastal conditions, including wind-driven rain, corrosion, and salt spray. Doors should have high-impact glass, full-perimeter nailing fins, a interlocking door seal between the fixed panel and the sliding door panel, and weather-stripping designed to prevent water intrusion. Doors need to be manufactured on the exterior side with materials that will not corrode, swell, crack, or rot. Fiberglass, aluminum, aluminum-clad, vinyl, and vinyl-clad doors with corrosive resistant hardware are good choices for the exterior sides of the door.

Screen mesh

Use safety glass or lexan.

The left photo shows a vinyl-clad sliding-glass patio door with a exterior sliding screen panel. **The insert photo** is a close-up of the exterior screen panel. For additional protection from wind-driven rain, remove the screen mesh from the panel and install clear Lexan or safety glass. Lexan weighs less than glass and will not shatter. A glass company can make the modification.

The insert photo at the right shows the custom safety-glass panel. When the sliding-glass panel is closed, it has the same function as a storm door. **Note:** *The sliding-glass panel should only be used for coastal storms, not for hurricane protection.*

23

Maintenance

Sliding patio doors are wonderful, as long as they slide easily and comfortably. Here are some simple maintenance tips that will enable your sliding patio door to function well throughout it's life:

Corroded angle bracket attached to the fixed panel of a sliding patio door. Removing rust stains, corroded screws, and hardware from this expensive door can be difficult.
Replace with a corrosive-resistant stainless steel or a non–metallic angle bracket.
Note: *When purchasing exterior doors make sure they are assembled with corrosive-resistant hardware from the manufacturer.*

Adjust the door rollers. Rollers should be made of materials that will not corrode. If your door is not level, it will not roll easily and may not latch and seal properly. This may allow for wind driven-rain to penetrate inside and damage the floor system.

Lubricate the track with a wax stick. Likewise, keep the rollers themselves lubricated with oil. The salt and sand in a coastal environment will always find a way into moving parts. Keep them clean, and lubricated to avoid expensive repairs and headaches!

Use a brass or stainless steel wire brush and vacuum to keep the track and bottom sill clean of dirt, sand, and debris. Make sure the track has not been damaged or bent so the door will operate and roll as it should.
Note: *Never use a carbon steel wire brush, to clean aluminum or stainless steel, it can leave a rust residue or may cause rust pitting on the track surface. Brass and stainless steel wire brushes can be purchased at a coastal hardware or home improvement store.*

This sliding patio door is designed with a weep system in the bottom sill to allow water to drain outside. Wind-driven rain will sometimes force its way between the fixed-door panel and the sliding-door panel. A sloped sill and a weep-hole system will divert water away if the water enters the bottom door sill. Keep the slotted drain hole free from debris; this will prevent water from over-flowing the inside track and damaging the floor system.
Note: *The photo is just one example how a manufacturer has address the problem of wind-driven rain entering between the fix panel and the sliding door panel. Before deciding on a sliding patio door for your coastal home, carefully investigate and evaluate how a particular door system has been designed, to prevent wind-driven rain from entering any part of the complete door assembly. A lesson learned... Reference the Coastal Products Directory.*

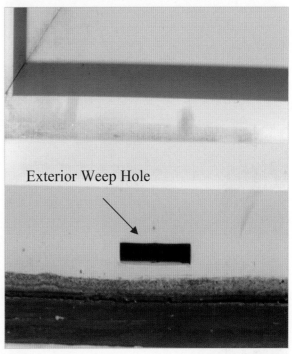

Exterior Weep Hole

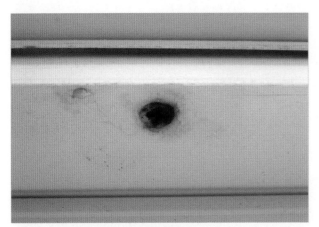

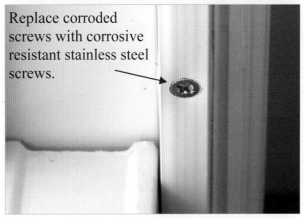

Replace corroded screws with corrosive resistant stainless steel screws.

If you see a screw head starting to rust or corrode, replace it immediately with a stainless steel screw, before its too late.(Take the opportunity to replace all metal-plated screws exposed to the salt-air at this time.) A lesson learned...

Entry Doors—Hinged

Severe winds are a serious concern. Choose a door that has been designed and tested duplicating hurricane-force winds, wind-driven rain, wind-blown debris, and other conditions. Door systems designed for coastal areas maximize the sill between the door and the frame to keep out the damaging effects of wind and rain. This also increases energy efficiency. The door will have a rein-forced frame and panel with a multi-point lock system and full-perimeter weather seals. Choose a door system that will not warp, rot, crack, peel, or split. Reference the Coastal Products Directory in the appendix section of this book.

French patio door: Aluminum construction, fully weather-stripped, with impact-resistant glass and corrosive-resistant hardware. (Photo courtesy of PGT Industries.)

French patio door: Whether in-swing or out-swing, choose a door that has been tested for coastal conditions, impact-resistant glass, and corrosive-resistant hardware that will not warp, swell, or rot. **Note:** *Out-swing doors are being used more often in coastal areas. High winds and wind-driven rain blowing against an out-swing door will force the door against perimeter door seals and weather stripping, creating a tighter seal, keeping out water intrusion. (Photo courtesy of Weather Shield MFG.)*

Storm doors will add another layer of protection against wind-driven rain and flying debris.

It is a simple fact that painted-steel doors will corrode in a coastal environment. Performing the kind of ongoing maintenance that would keep you ahead of the "corrosion curve" is tiring and, ultimately, futile. When choosing a door, your best, long-term choice is a fiberglass, aluminum, aluminum-clad, vinyl or vinyl-clad with stainless steel or solid-brass hinges and screws. Add a stainless steel or a solid-brass doorknob and deadbolt and you will have an attractive door that will work well for many years. A lesson learned...

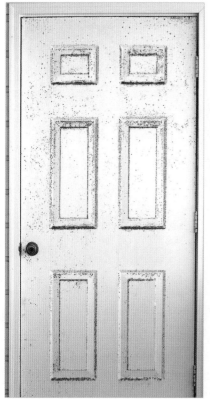

Left photo: Corroded galvanized-steel entrance door with a corroded metal-plated entry lock.

Right photo: Fiberglass entrance door that will not warp, corrode, rot, or swell in a coastal environment. This door also has corrosive-resistant entry hardware designed for the salt-air environment.

Left photo: The salt-air environment has corroded the bottom of this galvanized-steel entrance door.

Right photo: A fiberglass entrance door with glass sidelights and transom that will not warp, swell, corrode, or rot. Installed with solid-brass entry hardware.

Garage Doors

How many times have you seen an attractive house, with a garage that looks a bit shabby and worn, as if it had been forgotten? Too often. The same care that is taken for the house should be extended to the garage itself—even if it's only used for storage.

First, the garage door needs to operate smoothly, whether it is electric or not. When the door is open, the corrosive air will enter the garage. Lubricate all moving parts annually.

Lubricate all moving parts, including roller bearings, door hinges, springs, and latches.

Inspect all garage-door seals. Garage-door seals are attached to the doorjambs and door header. They are designed to overlap the door to prevent water intrusion caused by wind-driven rain. The 15 minutes you spend on this task today can save you a great deal of aggravation and money later.

 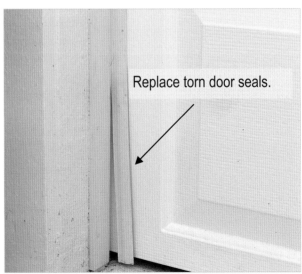

Corroded galvanized-metal garage door with a deteriorating door seal.

Inspect and replace damaged garage-door seals to prevent water intrusion from wind-driven rain.

As for the garage door itself, you will find that most doors are manufactured from the following materials: wood, metal, vinyl, and high-density polyethylene (HDPE). Vinyl and HDPE requires the least maintenance in the coastal environment. **Note:** *Depending on location, local building codes may require a garage door to meet a specific wind-rated design pressure, (DP) rating. We will discuss (DP) ratings later in this chapter. Reference the Coastal Products Directory.*

A vinyl garage door. Vinyl or HDPE garage doors are the best low-maintenance choice and will not corrode. A lesson learned...

As you can see from the photos, a galvanized-metal garage door will quickly rust and corrode in a coastal environment. In order to keep it looking good, you will have to sand, prime, and paint frequently, using anti-rust, oil based paint.

See enlarged photo below

Wood garage doors will often require frequent maintenance and repair to refinish or repaint every few years. You will also find that wood panels can swell, crack, and rot. Again the best choice is a vinyl or HDPE garage door. They require less maintenance and will not rot, swell, corrode, or require painting.

The close up photo on the right shows a wood garage door panel swollen due to moisture. There is evidence of wood damage that leaves it vulnerable to additional moisture intrusion.

Wood rot on a garage door panel

Windows

For your windows to be a joy and provide you with light, air, and protection, you need to consider materials and installation. Few things are as frustrating as a window that leaks in a coastal storm, requiring frequent maintenance, or one that will not easily open or close. Wind-driven rain will find a way inside, damaging carpet, and causing wood rot and other problems. Not all windows are designed for high winds and wind-driven rain. Not all windows have corrosive-resistant hardware with high-impact laminated glass.

Whether double-hung or casement, choose your windows carefully, making informed choices that will keep the coastal elements outside, allowing you to enjoy years of maintenance-free performance.

Traditionalists sometimes argue for "natural" materials when it comes to anything about a house. But when it comes to the problems of swollen and warped windows or rotted sills caused by water intrusion, it's time to draw the line.

You may accept that wood will need to be maintained with more diligence than vinyl, fiberglass, or aluminum. But that presumes with maintenance, it will continue to perform as well as these other materials. It won't.

Top left photo: Twin vinyl double-hung window with grilles between the glass panes.

Bottom left Photo: Vinyl double-hung window with grilles between the glass panes. Vinyl windows will not swell, warp, or corrode. **Note:** *Make sure your windows have been tested for wind-driven rain and have impact-resistant glass.*

Vinyl-clad casement window. Vinyl windows will not rot, swell, or corrode in a coastal environment.

Wood windows and wood trim are not recommended in a coastal environment.

Replace wood window trim with vinyl, treated wood, composite, cellular PVC or fiber-cement window trim.

Wood collects moisture causing it to warp, swell, and rot. All this diminishes the beauty and function of your windows and makes them nearly impossible to actually use. Years ago, I read that the closer you live to the coast, the more wood belongs in the woods!

Maintenance

As with sliding patio doors, the moving parts of a casement window require regular maintenance, as shown in the photographs. By providing this simple maintenance, your windows will last years longer. Some manufacturers will offer a coastal hardware package with stainless steel hardware as an option for windows installed in coastal areas.

The top and bottom linkages on your casement windows should be cleaned and lubricated annually to maintain a smooth operation throughout the life of your window.

Installation

Coastal environments often have slashing, wind-driven rains. For this reason, the method of window and door installation is as important as the choice of window and door itself—if you hope to preserve the beauty and function of your home. Manufacturers are required by code to provide structural installation details. Your installer should study and follow the installation instructions carefully. The structural fastening system of a door or window is designed to transfer the force of the impact and wind pressure to the surrounding wall system. **Note:** *Before installing windows and doors, consult with your local building inspector for the latest code requirements.*

Inadequate weatherproofing of doors and windows is common. Coastal areas have day-to-day wind and water exposure that will cause failure if good moisture management practices are not followed. Lack of weatherproofing will result in wood rot in the wall and floor systems. Wood rot may not be covered under your homeowner's insurance policy. When installing a window, follow these steps to avoid this problem:

1. Install adhesive flashing on all window and door openings as moisture barrier.

2. Install 30–pound felt or breathable house wrap as a moisture barrier.

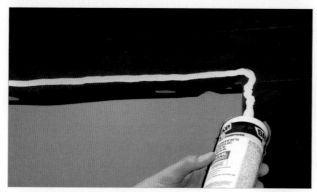

3. Apply a premium silicone caulking around the rough opening where the window fins will be attached.

4. Install the window and apply adhesive flashing over the window fins to seal out moisture.

The installer should never overlook moisture-management details. As the photographs show, the proper preparation and installation can be the difference between a perfect window and a disaster. **Note:** *As a added precaution against wood rot caused by water intrusion, you can also install pressure treated or water resistant sheathing and framing around all window and door openings A lesson learned...*

Additional Moisture-Management Practices

Sill Pans

Sill-pan flashing provides protection against water leakage around the seal and framing of doors and windows. Install by adhering the sill pan to the top or bottom of the rough opening for a door or window. **Note:** *Sill pans direct moisture away from doors and windows to prevent moisture from getting to interior surfaces.* Sill pans are inexpensive molded plastic, impervious to rust, corrosion, and will not deteriorate. Reference the manufacture's instructions before installing.

 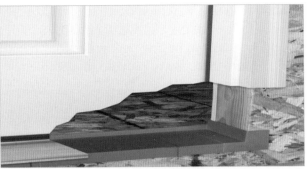

The left photo shows a sill pan installed in the rough opening of a window. **The right photo** shows a cut-away of a sill pan installed beneath a door unit. Reference the Coastal Products Directory. Photos courtesy of Jamsill Guard. **Note:** *Coastal building codes may require the use of sill pans in your area.*

House Wrap

House wraps are a water proof barrier. Install over the sheathing and behind the exterior siding. Siding can be vinyl siding, wood clapboard, vinyl shakes, or brick facade. House wrap is the last line of defense in stopping incoming water or exterior water condensation from getting into the wooden stud wall. If moisture gets behind a window, door, or siding, and is allowed to build-up within the stud or cavity walls, mold, wood rot, and termites can cause serious damage. Coastal homes are especially vulnerable to moisture intrusion caused by wind-driven rain. Typical house wraps include asphalt saturated felt or house wraps from varies synthetic materials.

The left photo shows a moisture-barrier house wrap with drainage channels that allow excess moisture to drain and exit the wall system.
Bottom photo: close-up view of "Rain Drop" house wrap with drain channels. Reference the Coastal Products Directory. (Photo courtesy of Pactiv Building Products.)

Impact Zone (IZ)

Windows, Doors, and the Coastal Environment

People who live along the coastal areas are familiar with hard, wind-driven rains. However, very often those winds become tropical-force; or even hurricane-force winds. In addition to the potential damage that wind and rain can cause, high winds often bring with them flying debris, tree branches, lawn furniture, or toys.

When flying debris penetrates a window or the glass pane on a door, disaster awaits. Once a window is broken or a doorway compromised, the interior of the house is vulnerable to the wind pressures and wind-driven rain.

Coastal zoning and building codes from Rhode Island to Florida to Texas now take into account the hazard of flying debris in a coastal environment. (Determining the required impact zone, either IZ2 , IZ3 or IZ4 window depends on where it is to be installed, "where" being determined by the code's wind-speed zones.) As a rule of thumb, the closer to the coast, the stronger the window needs to be. For example, wind zone 4, closest to the coast is rated for 140+ miles per hour.

When choosing windows and doors for your home, anticipate this kind of hazard. There are a number of double-strength windows that use reinforced, tempered, impact-resistant glass that protect your home from flying debris. These windows have the added benefit of providing a secure noise barrier, energy efficiency, and added safety from intruders. Reference the Coastal Products Directory.

Broken glass without reinforced lamination.

Re-enforced laminated glass. Note how the laminated glass shards hold together, keeping out wind and rain and reducing the potential hazard of sharp broken glass.

Energy Performance Label for Doors or Windows

The energy performance label located on a new door or window can help you determine how well the product will perform. The following values addressed on the energy performance label will help you when comparing products. All data is courtesy of the National Fenestration Rating Council (NFRC) and Window and Door Manufactures Association (WDMA).

1 U-Factor
The U-factor measures how well a product prevents heat from escaping. The rate of heat loss is indicated in terms of the U-factor (U-value) of a window assembly. The U-factor rating will be between 0.20 and 1.20. The lower the U-value, the greater resistance to heat flow and the better insulating value.

2 Solar Heat-Gain Coefficient
The solar heat-gain coefficient measures how well a product blocks heat cause by sunlight. This is expressed by a number between 0 and 1. The lower the solar heat-gain coefficient, the less solar heat transmits into the house.

3 Visible Transmittance
The visible transmittance (VT) measures how much light comes through a product. VT is expressed as a number between 0 and 1. The higher the VT, the more light is transmitted.

4 Air Leakage
Air Leakage (AL) is indicated by an air-leakage rating, expressed as the equivalent cubic foot of air passing through a square foot of window area: (cfm/sq.ft). Heat loss and gain occur by infiltration through cracks in the window assembly. The lower the AL, the less air leakage.

5 Condensation Resistance (Optional test not required.)
Condensation resistance (CR) measures the ability to resist the formation of condensation on the interior surface of the product. The higher the CR rating, the better that product is at resisting condensation formation. The CR is expressed as a number between 0 and 100.

6 Window and Door Manufactures Association (WDMA) Hallmark certification
Indicates the window, door or skylight has met all WDMA air infiltration resistance, water penetration resistance and structural performance tests and is a mark of excellence in the industry. Coastal homeowners should know a higher performance grade (PG) or design pressure (DP) rating indicates the product has passed higher performance requirements.

1) DP40 window or door was tested for structural integrity with a wind speed up to 155 MPH.

2) DP50 window or door was tested for structural integrity with a wind speed up to 173 MPH.

Wind Zone 4 lets you know the window or door can be installed in all locations with winds greater than 140 mph. Missile level D impact test, qualifies the product for basic protection in wind zone 1,2,3,4 for building less than or equal to 30 feet in height. **Note:** *Contact your local building inspection department for window, door and skylight requirements in your area.*

Make sure your window or door has a label that states it meets ENERGY STAR® guidelines for energy efficiency.

National Fenestration Rating Council ®
CERTIFIED

World's Best Window Co.

Millennium 2000+
Vinyl-Clad Wood Frame
Double Glazing • Argon Fill • Low E
Product Type: **Vertical Slider**

ENERGY PERFORMANCE RATINGS

	U-Factor (U.S./I-P)		Solar Heat Gain Coefficient
1	**0.35**	2	**0.32**

ADDITIONAL PERFORMANCE RATINGS

	Visible Transmittance		Air Leakage (U.S./I-P)
3	**0.51**	4	**0.2**
5	Condensation Resistance **51**		—

Manufacturer stipulates that these ratings conform to applicable NFRC procedures for determining whole product performance. NFRC ratings are determined for a fixed set of environmental conditions and a specific product size. NFRC does not recommend any product and does not warrant the suitability of any product for any specific use. Consult manufacturer's literature for other product performance information.
www.nfrc.org

WINDOW & DOOR MANUFACTURERS ASSOCIATION **WDMA** 6 **Hallmark Certified** www.wdma.com	Licensee: XXX-H-XXX [or] ABC Window Company Casement Window Series 100 Manufacturer Stipulates Conformance as indicated below
STANDARD	**RATING**
AAMA/WDMA/CSA 101/I.S.2/A440-08	Class R-PG50: Size tested 760 × 1520 mm (30 × 60 in) -Type C DP +50/-65
ASTM E1996-02 / ASTM E1886-02	Wind Zone 4, Missile Level D, Design Pressure +50/-50 psf

3

Exterior Siding and Trim

A *well-maintained waterfront property. The white PVC trim on this home will not warp, rot, or absorb moisture, and never needs painting. PVC uses the same carpentry techniques as wood— cuts, mills, shapes, routs like wood, and easy to custom finish. Photo courtesy of Versatex PVC trim products. Reference the Coastal Products Directory.*

This chapter will give the coastal homeowner low-maintenance options when choosing an exterior siding. These siding products are high-wind rated, durable, and will not require painting. Included are valuable installation techniques that take into consideration high winds, wind-driven rain, and siding tear-off caused by coastal storms.

This Chapter Includes
Low Maintenance Siding Products
Exterior Trim Products
Siding Installation

Beauty is only skin deep. What we see is what we deem beautiful. The exterior surface of your house is the way that you present your home to the world. You want your home to reflect its value and beauty in this most obvious way.

For years, cedar shake (a very hardy wood) was the "skin" of choice for beach cottages. However, over time, the cedar shake would warp or curl, stain or grow mold, or become mildewed. If it was painted, it needed to be painted over and over—the same as all other wood products in a coastal environment.

Natural wood-shake shingle siding.

Still, cedar shakes were responsible for the "cottage" look that for many years, particularly in the northeast, people associated with coastal homes. As the population in coastal areas grew, manufacturer's developed low-maintenance siding designed and tested to withstand hurricane-force winds. Coastal homes began to reflect different materials and colors.

Low-Maintenance Siding

Several options include polymer and vinyl shakes—vinyl siding insulated with rigid foam backing, composite-fiber cement and masonry products. Fortunately, the materials that have been developed have made siding more durable, color fast, natural looking, and attractive as an exterior choice for homeowners. Most are available with a high-wind rating and long-term finish warranties against fading because the color is not just a finish but is completely through the product. Reference the Coastal Products Directory.

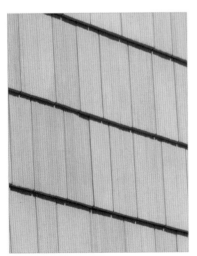

Vinyl, polymer-shake siding. Available in many colors. With high-wind rating.

Composite fiber-cement siding. Available primed or painted.

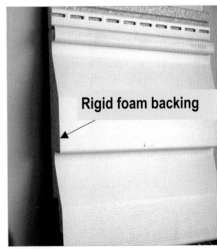

Rigid foam-backed insulated vinyl siding. Available in many colors. With high-wind rating.

The left photo above shows a home with insulated rigid-foam back vinyl siding and True Texture rough-cedar exterior finish. Virtually maintenance free, never needs painting even in a coastal salt-air environment. The paint color is completely through the product. Rigid-foam backing can increase overall thermal performance helping to reduce heating and cooling costs. This product is designed and tested for hurricane-force winds, the exterior surface is impact resistant.

The right photo above shows fiber-cement siding. The siding is moisture, termite, and impact-resistant. Has the traditional look of wood with lower maintenance. (Both photos courtesy of CertainTeed Corp.) Reference the Coastal Products Directory.

This coastal home has vinyl polymer-shake siding with a rough cedar-shake style appearance. Virtually maintenance free with the color completely through the shake. It never needs painting. Has been designed and tested for hurricane-force winds. Will not warp or rot. (Photo courtesy of CertainTeed Corp.) Reference the Coastal Products Directory.

Exterior Trim Products (Low Maintenance)

The left photo shows a home with fiber-cement trim boards. Prime on all six sides, moisture resistant, termite resistant, and noncombustible. (Photo courtesy of Plycem, Inc.) **The right photo** shows a home with white cellular PVC trim boards that will not warp, rot, or absorb moisture. (Photo courtesy of Certain Teed Corp.) Both photos reflect low-maintenance trim boards. Reference the Coastal Products Directory.

Siding Installation

By measuring and planning ahead and using longer lengths of siding the contractor eliminated all vertical seams on the side wall of this house.

Standard sidings are typically 12ft. long. Seams appear every two to three feet. Longer–length sidings are offered in 16ft. and 20ft. lengths. The primary benefit of longer-length siding panels is that they reduce the number of vertical seams in the wall. This reduces the possibility of tear-off and water intrusion caused by high winds and wind-driven rain. **Note:** *Siding shall be installed per the manufacture's installation instruction and coastal building code requirements*. (Photo courtesy of CertainTeed Corp.) Reference the Coastal Products Directory.

Oceanfront, oceanside, and soundside homes covered with lightweight, hollow vinyl siding can have problems with blow-off if not installed properly. This could lead to wood rot, termite infestation, and structural damage if not addressed immediately. This type of vinyl siding requires vertical lap seams, as shown in the photo. Never install vinyl siding with the vertical lap seams facing the ocean or sound side winds. High winds can get behind the lap seams, peel back or blow-off the siding.

Never assume your siding contractor will consider the prevailing wind direction when installing lightweight vinyl siding.

Vinyl siding with the vertical lap seams facing toward the oceanside winds. Strong oceanside winds have peeled back and separated the vinyl siding, allowing for water intrusion.

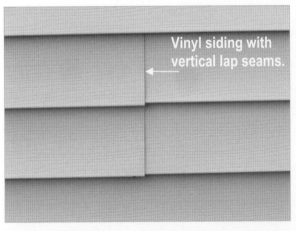

Vinyl siding with vertical lap seams.

As we have discussed by measuring, planning ahead, and using longer lengths of siding, you can minimize the number of vertical lap seams in your project. Reducing vertical lap seams on exterior siding will minimize the possibility of water intrusion cause by wind-driven rain. It may also prevent other maintenance issues especially in a coastal environment.

Siding seams can be an aesthetic objection to vinyl siding. Longer lengths can also reduce the amount of labor required to install siding, since more area can be covered with fewer panels.

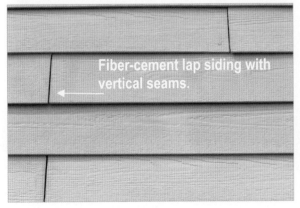

Fiber-cement lap siding with vertical seams.

Siding seams should not have wide unsealed gaps as shown in the photo. The gap size should be 1/8" to 1/4" maximum. To repair and seal the gaps, insert a small thin piece of noncorrosive flashing material behind the gap and flush with the horizontal lap seam. The flashing material needs to be several times wider than the gap to prevent moisture or water from damaging the sheathing and wall studs. Next, use a premium exterior silicone paintable caulk to fill the gap in order to seal out moisture or water intrusion.

4

Coastal Heating and Cooling

S *and in the fins and excessive corrosion on your heat pumps (condenser units) can affect the performance, reduce the life of the unit, and lead to thousands of dollars in replacement cost.*

For most homeowners, replacing a heating and cooling system is not something that must be done very often; for the coastal homeowner living in a salt-air environment, if the environment is not taken into account, the heating and cooling system will not last. It is a substantial investment, and it pays to research and shop wisely before making a decision. **Smart choices save money.**

This chapter will give valuable information as to what you should look for before choosing a new heating and cooling system. It will show how care and maintenance will extend the life of your heating and cooling system in a salt-air environment, saving thousands of dollars.

This Chapter Includes

Preventing corrosion
Air-handling Units
Care and Maintenance
Floor Registers

Ultimately, you want to be comfortable in your home. That means making sure that the interior environment is comfortable. Generally, people move to the coast because of the coastal region's temperate climate—cooler in the summer and milder in the winter than that of interior regions. There are plenty of times, however, when just opening the windows and allowing the ocean breeze to blow in is not enough. At those times, you will need either heating or air-conditioning, depending on the season.

Heating, ventilating, and air-conditioning (HVAC) refers to the technology for controlling the interior environment. HVAC can be as simple as a handful of electric heaters and window-mounted air-conditioning units or as complex and efficient as a central unit that controls numerous zones to maximize comfort throughout your coastal home. Central HVAC includes an outside heat pump with a cabinet containing a condenser coil and compressor and an indoor evaporator coil (air handler unit).

Coastal environments are characterized by salt spray. Even if your home is a number of miles inland, wind, fog, and sea mist can carry the salt and cause corrosion. Obviously, the closer your home is to the coast, the more significant the salt content. In addition, the relative humidity of the environment will impact how corrosive the environment is to your unit. As a guide, take a walk through the neighborhood near your home and look at the condenser units. Take note of the corrosion occurring on the units.

These Condenser units exposed to the coastal environment exhibit excessive corrosion on the cabinets. Internal corrosion will affect the performance and reduce the life of the unit.

Not long ago, wall-mounted or window-mounted, single-room air conditioners were the primary method for cooling rooms and removing humidity from inside the house. While these are still in use, and demand the same kind of consideration as the central units we will discuss, they do not represent the same investment as the central units, which are more efficient and manage the interior environment of your entire home.

Preventing Corrosion

Window air-conditioning units will corrode if exposed to the salt-air environment.

Apply a marine-grade corrosion inhibitor to the cabinet of the window air-conditioning unit to minimize corrosion build-up. **Note:** *When the unit is not being used, install a protective cover over the cabinet to prevent corrosion.*

As we have seen with every component we have examined, using certain metals is an invitation to rust and corrosion. Inferior materials and units will cause you to suffer more cost, headaches, and aggravation than comfort. As with all things, get it right from the beginning, and your life will be much more satisfying.

Corrosion in the condenser units is the primary cause of equipment failure, which is a common occurrence in a coastal environment when the units are not protected or maintained.

47

Both of these heat pumps (condenser units), have salt spray approved finishes.
Left photo shows a unit with a stainless steel cabinet.
Right photo shows a unit with a heavy gauge galvanized metal cabinet, with a powder-paint finish. Other positive features to consider when evaluating a condenser unit, does the unit have corrosive resistant copper tubes and a condenser guard to protect the coils from being damaged by flying debris?

Always look for heat pumps (condenser units) which are coated on both the exterior and interior components of the unit with special corrosive-resistant coatings. **Note**: *Factory warranty, equipment performance, equipment cost, and especially customer service should always be a primary consideration when evaluating a HVAC system for your coastal home. (Right photo above is courtesy of Amana Heating and Air Conditioning.) Reference the Coastal Products Directory.*

Also consider building an appropriate enclosure for your condenser unit(s). Not only will an enclosure add to the beauty of your home, but it will also offer additional protection from the sun, the wind, salt spray, and wind-driven sand, thereby extending the life and effectiveness of the unit. The photo below shows a simple enclosure built to protect the condenser units. **Note**: *In accordance with flood zone requirements, coastal building codes may require condensers be located on a raised or elevated platform. Elevating the condensers on a platform above ground will protect them from rising water, it also exposes them to even more salt spray, wind-driven rain, and flying debris. Consider building an enclosure, attaching it to the elevated platform, similar to the enclosure in the photo. When building an elevated platform with an enclosure, make sure your contractor considers high winds from coastal storms, requirements from the manufacturer, and local building codes.*

Air-Handling Units (AHU)

Air-handling units (AHU) are used to condition and circulate the air as part of a heating, ventilating, and air-conditioning system. When installing an AHU inside your home, consider placing the unit in a conditioned space to prolong the life of the unit. Often, AHUs are placed in attics; most attics are not conditioned spaces, so humidity, salt-air, salt-moisture will migrate through the attic ventilation, reducing the life of the unit. Because of this, the AHU may corrode faster than the condenser unit sitting outside. Have your AHU serviced annually.

An air-handling unit installed in an unconditioned attic space will corrode in a salt-air environment.

Care and Maintenance

In order to stay warm and cozy, not only does your house have to be adequately sealed, (which we will discuss in another chapter), your heating system must also be working efficiently.

The extent with which you can keep sand and salt mist from collecting in your unit corresponds with its longevity. Even if you have chosen the appropriate unit(s) made of corrosive-resistant materials and with corrosive-resistant coatings, it is still a good idea to regularly rinse off the cabinet to clean away any salt mist or sand that may have collected on the fins and coil or other exposed components inside the unit.

Rinse off salt mist and sand with fresh water frequently to minimize corrosion on the cabinet, fins, coils, and internal components. This practice will extend the life of the outside condenser unit.

Rinsing off salt mist and sand with fresh water can be done with a garden hose or by adding a pop-up sprinkler head that sprays the condenser unit each time the lawn is irrigated.

Pop-up sprinkler timed to come on with the lawn sprinklers.

Spray on a water-resistant, marine-grade corrosion inhibitor to minimize exterior corrosion.

Make sure your HVAC contractor has personnel who can respond quickly to a service call and a qualified technician to evaluate and service the heating and cooling system annually.

Floor Registers

The damp salt environment will corrode metal floor registers which can damage all types of flooring. Use registers made from non-corroding materials.

Corroded metal floor registers will quickly stain carpet and other types of flooring.

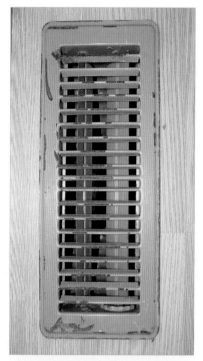

Corroded metal floor register will leave rust stains on hardwood flooring.

Carpet is permanently damaged by the rust from the corroded floor register in the top photo.

Plastic floor register will not corrode. **Note:** *Both plastic and wood floor registers can be purchased at a coastal hardware or home improvement store.*

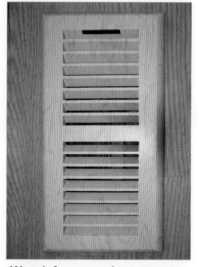

Wood, faux wood, or noncorrosive floor registers will not rust or permanently stain the flooring.

5

Exterior Electrical Components

A noncorrosive, weather tight exterior light fixture with a sealed bulb to keep out salt moisture and wind-driven rain. Reference the Coastal Products Directory.

When we turn on an exterior deck or floodlight, we expect the light to come on. If it does not, we assume the bulb is blown, and we replace it. In a coastal area, a bad light bulb may not be the only problem. Salt moisture can enter the fixture as a result of wind-driven rain, corroding the internal light socket, causing the breaker inside your electrical panel box to trip, shutting off the power to the light and other electrical components. If moisture inside the fixture is not addressed, it may cause a more serious electrical problem.

In this chapter you will learn what you should consider when choosing an appropriate exterior light fixture. We will show how certain tips and techniques will prevent moisture from getting into your exterior electrical components.

Finally, no homeowner wants to replace a meter-base enclosure. It is costly, requiring coordination between several entities and a temporary power outage. You will be introduced to corrosion-resistant meter-base enclosures that will last years longer in a coastal environment and save you time, money, and frustration.

This Chapter Includes
Coastal Exterior Lighting
Door Bells
Sealing Out Moisture
Meter-Base Enclosures

Coastal Exterior Lighting

Stroll down a street in a beach community after the sun has set and you will see exterior lights on the houses that not only provide security, but also show off the houses in a soft, inviting way. This is very different from how the house looks in the sunlight.

However, if upon closer inspection, those exterior lights and other electrical fixtures show signs of rust and corrosion, the attractiveness of the house is diminished and quite possibly, the function of the fixtures is compromised—allowing for water intrusion and wood rot.

Non-corroding light fixtures designed for the coastal environment. Although not all non-corroding fixtures are sealed, sealed fixtures are the best choice. Reference the Coastal Products Directory.

 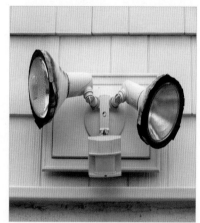 

Deteriorated flood and exterior lighting are not suited for the salt-air environment. To prevent water intrusion from wind-driven rain the best choice is a sealed light fixture made from materials that will not corrode. A lesson learned...

 ## Door Bells

Ding Dong... Who's Calling?

Whether a simple bell or the first three bars of a symphony, doorbells announce the arrival of guests and visitors in a way that is charming and fun. But if the doorbell presents itself in an unattractive manner—old, chipped, cracked, or corroded—then it suggests to your guests and visitors that maybe your home is not all that inviting after all. Just as we advised for other hardware, pay attention to materials. Also, when it comes to electrical components, bear in mind that corrosion is not simply ugly; but it can render the item unusable and can cause a safety hazard.

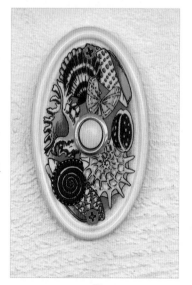 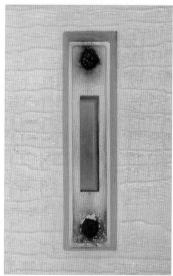

Rather than the simple plastic doorbell with plated screws that will deteriorate, consider a doorbell that will not corrode, and secure it with stainless steel screws.

Sealing Out Moisture

If there is one word to keep in mind when it comes to exterior electrical lighting and receptacles, it is "sealed." Exposed lighting and receptacles allow moisture and salt-air in. The more protected they are from moisture and the elements—as the photographs make clear—the safer and more attractive they remain. Taking these extra steps will keep wind-driven rain from entering and damaging the fixtures during coastal storms.

Use a premium-grade silicone caulk.

A sealed fluorescent floodlight installed with stainless steel screws and caulked between the fixture and the soffit.

A sealed, wall-mounted deck light installed with stainless steel screws and caulked between the light fixture and the exterior siding.

Below, and on the following page, are some additional actions you can take to give your electrical components maximum protection:

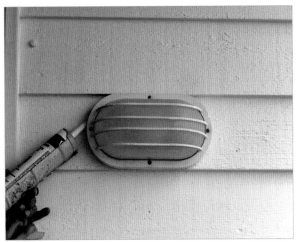

1. Use a premium-grade silicone caulking to caulk around all exterior lighting and receptacles.

 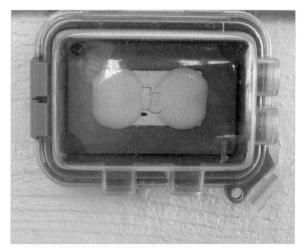

2. Install child-safety plugs for additional protection against moisture and water intrusion.

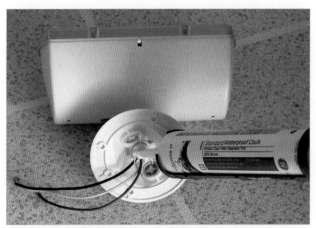

3. If your flood light is located near a continuous soffit vent, use silicone caulking to fill the hole in the mounting plate to prevent wind–driven rain and moisture from entering the wiring cavity and fixture.

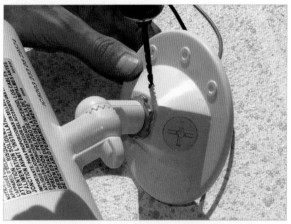

4. Drill "weep holes" to allow water to drain from the base of the floodlights when installed near a continuous soffit vent.

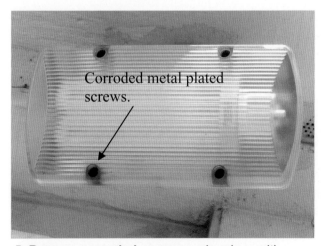

Corroded metal plated screws.

5. Remove corroded screws and replace with stainless steel screws.

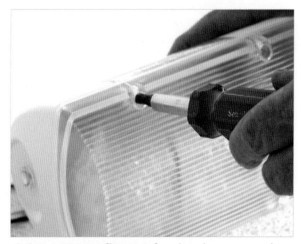

6. Inspect new fixtures for plated screws and replace with stainless steel screws.

Meter-Base Enclosures

The costly process of changing out a meter-base enclosure requires the homeowner to coordinate many steps. This procedure may vary depending on your municipality requirements. It generally involves a licensed electrician, the utility company, and the local authority (building inspection department). The utility company will disconnect the power source to the house (utility pole or transformer). The utility company will then remove the glass meter from the meter-base enclosure. The electrician will disconnect the wiring from the meter-base enclosure and remove the corroded galvanized meter-base enclosure, install the new meter-base enclosure, reconnect the wiring, and then notify the electrical inspector. Once the new enclosure has passed inspection, the inspector will notify the utility company. The utility company will reconnect the power service to the house and install the glass meter. The electrician will turn on the main power breaker in the house and verify that all the circuits are functional. **Note:** *The municipality may supply the new meter-base enclosure at a cost to you.* The smart choice is to replace it with a UL-rated corrosive-resistant aluminum meter-base enclosure made to resist salt air, salt spray.

A powder-coated or painted, aluminum meter-base enclosure will last years longer than a galvanized meter-base enclosure. Reference the Coastal Products Directory. **Note:** *When building a new home in a coastal area especially oceanside or soundside locations, route copper wiring to your meter base enclosure. Aluminum wiring can corrode, deteriorate and possibly break where the wiring strands terminates inside the meter base enclosure.*

When exposed to the salt-air and salt spray, galvanized meter-base enclosures will corrode and deteriorate costing time and money to replace. A lesson learned...

6

Coastal Decks

A place to relax and enjoy the view with family and friends, the coastal deck is an extension of your home.

A coastal home's entry is not limited to the front door. The closer a home is to the ocean or sound, the more likely it is to have extensive decking that leads to multiple entrances. The ocean and or sound view is an important asset to the value of your home. Coastal decks are a substantial investment, requiring careful planning of design and material construction. A deck must withstand the effects of coastal storms, the salt-air environment, and the wear and tear of normal use. To help you plan wisely, we will explore the advantages and disadvantages of real wood versus composite wood in a coastal area.

This chapter will introduce you to the various applications of pressure-treated wood. We will also give you valuable information when considering deck hardware and flashing requirements.

This Chapter Includes
Real Wood or Composite
Deck Flashing
Elevated Decks
Deck Hardware
Coastal Awnings

A deck on your coastal home is an extension of your living space. It will bring years of enjoyment, creating enjoyable spaces to sit and relax, enjoy the view, and entertain friends. A deck can transform your home and increase your property value. Flip through any architectural magazine, and you will find images of the deck, showing what it means to live in the house, whether overlooking a fine garden, a lake, or the ocean.

Like every other aspect of a home in a coastal area, a deck demands strict awareness and respect for the coastal environment. The materials used in its construction, the hardware used to build it, and even its physical layout need to be considered. The deck can be a sizable investment. Coastal decks are often elevated with multiple levels, and they often define a coastal home's appearance. Make uninformed choices in any of these areas, and your lesson learned will be a very expensive one. Make wise, informed choices, and your deck will be a source of comfort and enjoyment for many years to come.

Real Wood or Composite

It wasn't that long ago that the only real "choices" for a deck material were treated pine, redwood, cedar, or a South American hardwood. Today, most decks are built with real wood. But now there are composites that often rival wood in their look and feel. Composite decking with a compatible handrail will give a unified appearance and is increasing in popularity. The first decision that you should make regarding your deck is what material you will use, real wood or a composite.

Composite decking secured with hidden fasteners for a clean appearance.

A treated-wood deck, recently pressure washed and sealed to bring back the beauty of the wood.

Each has advantages and disadvantages that you should consider when making your decision. The simple truth is, natural wood has a character that is not easily matched by composite decking. That does not mean that wood is the better choice. Wood demands more maintenance than composite. Higher-grade hardwoods have greater durability than softer woods, but they are also more expensive.

The ultimate advantage to wood is that it is beautiful. If you maintain your wood deck appropriately, it will age gracefully and beautifully. Most woods are less expensive than composites. Your wood deck can be repaired, refinished, or repainted as needed, without the worry that a particular color or style has been discontinued.

Those same advantages are also wood deck's disadvantages, if you maintain it. That could prove to be a very big "if." Wood decks require annual maintenance and need to be sealed, stained, or painted every few years. Coastal storms can deteriorate the finish on wood decks. While their initial cost is lower than composites, wood tends to cost more over the life of the deck.

Wood decks can easily be repaired.

Wood decks require annual maintenance, consisting of staining, painting, or sealing.

Wood splinters, splits, cracks, and warps, which mean deck boards will need to be replaced.

Composites, which are usually a blend of wood fiber and plastic resin, are durable and low-maintenance. They are mold, mildew, pest, and rot resistant and do not have knots that can split and crack. However, they are not maintenance-free.

Composite decking secured with corrosive-resistant, square-head stainless steel screws.

Some composite decks can be painted but most cannot. Why paint a composite deck? It will only add to ongoing maintenance. Invest in a deck system with a good warranty. Potential issues with composite may be surface fading and stains.

On the downside, composite is generally more expensive than wood. Some composites may not be as strong as wood and can flex and sag; closer joist spacing may be recommended. During the hot summer months, some composite decking may retain heat and be hot to walk on with bare feet. Your deck will hold up only as long as the wood framing structure and deck hardware holds up. Decking products must be installed according to the manufacturer's recommendations. If not, you may void your warranty.

Some composite decking manufacturers may recommend closer joist spacing to prevent sag and flex of deck boards.

Which way to go?

The decision is yours and it rests more on a number of personal preferences rather than a firm, objective "better" or "best."

Composite decking secured with hidden fasteners can be cut and installed the same as wood.

Some manufactures have matching handrails available in composite or PVC material. Reference the Coastal Products Directory.

Composite

Composite decks and railings do stand up well to the coastal environment and, in some ways, outperform wood. Composite products are available in several shades of gray, white, and browns. Deeper graining and grooves have improved the surface textures, including smooth, wood-grain and other distinct patterns. Hidden fasteners add to the smooth appearance. Some composite planks are flexible enough to be easily cut and manipulated into patterns and shapes. Some composite decking comes available with anti-skid surfaces.

And while composites are often touted as "lasting forever" there is a difference between lasting forever and looking beautiful outside your home forever. Composite decking will need to be cleaned with mild detergent or with an approved deck cleaner. Unapproved chemicals may damage the finish and void the warranty. A final note about composite decks, evaluate several samples from your local home improvement store before committing to one product.

Wood (Pressure-Treated)

Pressure-treated wood has been used for many years in the construction of decks. Pressure treated wood is strong, resistant to decay, and resistant to termite infestation. Pressure treated wood is durable and easy to work with, has widespread availability, and is inexpensive. Not all wood is pressure-treated equally. Since January 1, 2004, almost all pressure treated wood sold in the United States has been produced with either ACQ (Alkaline Copper Quatemary) or CA (Copper Azole). These are arsenic-free treatments.

Different applications for pressure-treated wood impose different hazards on wood and require different amounts of preservatives for protection. These amounts are know as "retention levels," referring to the amounts of preservatives (pounds per cubic foot) retained in the wood after treatment. As a coastal homeowner, be sure to purchase wood treated for the intended application. The intended use is identified by the tag stapled to the end piece of the lumber. **Note:** *Retention levels may vary depending on supplier.*

1. .25 lbs. PCF—rated for use above ground only, e.g. deck planks and handrails.
2. .40 lbs. PCF—for use in ground contact, floor joist.
3. .60 lbs. PCF—for use in burying deck post in the ground.
4. .80 lbs. PCF—rated for marine use: freshwater contact, docks, and piers.
5. 2.50 lbs. PCF—rated for marine use: saltwater contact, docks, and piers.

Deck Flashing

Coastal decks that are bolted and secured to the house require a special connection and flashing detail. The connection will include pressure treated lumber, flashing, nails, and hardware. This critical deck-to-house connection is governed by local building codes. Flashing creates a moisture barrier between the deck and the house. Proper flashing will ensure that wind-driven rain will not make contact with your untreated house framing (i.e., flashing made of stainless steel, copper, vinyl, or a bituminous rubberized product). If the building code allows use a non-metallic material, consider "Vycor Deck Flashing," manufactured by W.R. Grace and Company. Installed behind a ledger board to protect the house sheathing from moisture intrusion A self-adhesive rubberized membrane, will self seal when penetrated by a bolt or fastener. Untreated house sheathing behind the ledger board is vulnerable to wood rot. Coastal building codes may require the house sheathing behind the ledger board to be pressure treated. **Note:** *Never use galvanized steel or aluminum flashing in a salt-air environment or in contact with ACQ pressure-treated wood. ACQ chemicals in the pressure-treated wood with the salt-air environment will cause these metals to deteriorate. Reference the Coastal Products Directory.*

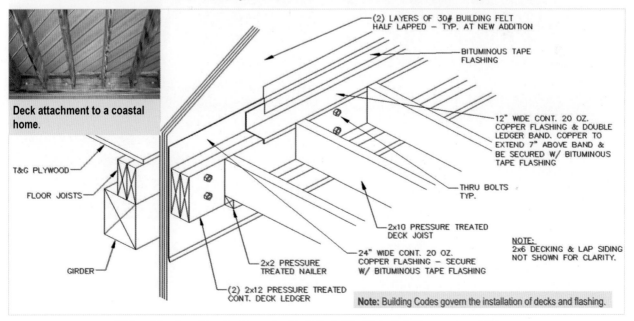

This drawing illustrates a typical deck flashing detail on a coastal home.

Elevated Decks

Coastal homes are often built and supported on pressure-treated pilings and may be multi-level. Each level may have a deck to relax and enjoy the summer breeze. Consider covering the exposed underside of the deck joist to give a cleaner, brighter, and more finished look, while also providing shelter from rain and water drainage. Reference the Coastal Products Directory.

The **exposed underside** of a deck does not allow for a clean appearance. Water will drain through and may create mold and mildew.

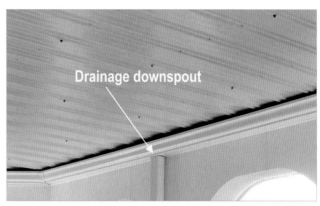

Drainage downspout

The **underside of a deck** that has been covered using an under-deck system that allows for drainage and gives the appearance of a clean, bright look.

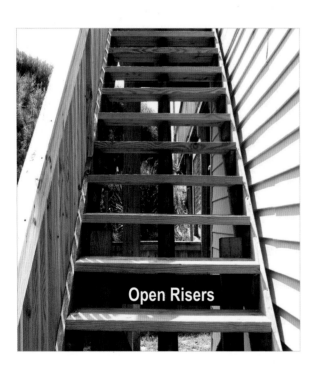

Open Risers

Closed Risers

Steps

The steps to your deck should have closed risers for added safety. While your local building codes will have the "final word" on matters such as this, even if they are not required, the closed risers will add to the safety and appearance.

Deck Hardware

What's good for the goose is good for the gander. What is true for screws and nails referenced in chapter one is good for deck hardware. Corrosion is the enemy!

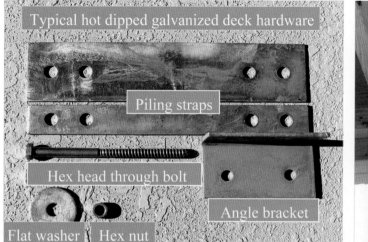

Decks are often assembled with hot dipped galvanized hardware. Metal straps, angles, hex head bolts, hex nuts, and flat washers are typical. **Left Photo:** Hot dipped galvanized deck connectors; piling straps, angle bracket, hex head through bolt, hex nuts, and flat washer. **Middle Photo:** Hot dipped galvanized piling strap, hex head through bolts, and hex nuts securing a support post to a deck band. **Right Photo:** Stainless steel piling strap, hex head through bolts, hex nuts and flat washers securing a support post to a floor girder. **Note:** *Manufacturer's will often design and fabricate specific deck hardware depending on the deck to deck or deck to house connection. Reference the Coastal Products Directory.*

Today, deck hardware has another corrosive enemy in coastal areas. Testing has shown that the new wood preservative ACQ is more corrosive to certain metals (e.g., galvanized metals and aluminum) than other preservatives. Use only hardware that has been approved for contact with ACQ-treated wood, such as stainless steel, or hot-dipped galvanized hardware. Hot-dipped galvanized bolts and straps are the minimum requirement. Hot-dipped galvanized hardware is very corrosion resistant but will corrode more quickly the closer it is to an oceanfront environment. Double hot-dipped galvanized is a better choice. If your budget allows, an upgrade would be stainless steel bolts and deck connectors. Consider using "Vycor Deck Flashing" as a barrier between the connectors to prevent corrosion from the ACQ chemicals in the lumber. Reference the Coastal Products Directory and follow the installation procedures outline on the product website.

The same applies to deck screws and fasteners. Use only the screws and fasteners approved for contact with ACQ pressure-treated wood. When compared to the overall cost of a deck project, the deck screws and fasteners are a very small cost.

Corrosive-resistant coated deck screws are approved for use with ACQ lumber.

Corrosive-resistant stainless steel deck screws are approved for use with ACQ lumber.

Corroded deck hardware affects the integrity of the entire deck structure and should be replaced immediately for the safety of everyone. **Note:** *Deck assembly and hardware are governed by local building codes.*

Corroded galvanized piling strap and hex bolts.

Corroded galvanized deck bolts and hex nuts.

Corroded galvanized piling strap and hex bolts.

Corroded galvanized joist hanger.

Coastal Awnings

Awnings provide protection from the hot summer sun by giving a deck shade and protection from the coastal elements. Coastal deck awnings must be corrosion-resistant, with and aluminum frame, retractable aluminum arms with stainless steel or PVC coated cables and assembled with stainless steel hardware, to have any chance in a salt-air environment. The awning should be lubricated often with an approved water and salt resistant lubricant.

Awnings are either manual or electric. I suggest electric awnings with a wind speed-sensor. The wind sensor triggers the awning to retract when the wind reaches the programmed set speed. With a wind-speed sensor you will not have to worry when summer storms occur quickly, the awning will automatically retract. This can save on a costly repair. Reference the Coastal Products Directory.

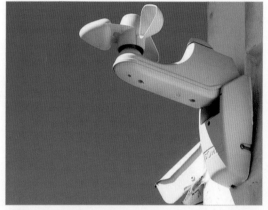

Wind speed sensor set to manufacturer's recommendations.

Maintain your awnings with a salt-resistant lubricant.

Awnings provide shade in the hot summer sun.

Inspect and re-caulk window trim, door trim, and corner boards.

Use a premium grade silicone caulk to seal small gaps in your siding.

Repair rusty nail heads prior to painting.

Replace split siding prior to painting to prevent moisture intrusion.

Inspect for soft spots. Repair wood rot prior to painting.

7

Exterior Surface Preparation

*C*oastal homes are often buffeted by high winds and wind-driven rain. The salt environment has weathered the exterior finish. This home is in need of exterior surface preparation prior to finishing with a premium severe-weather paint or stain.

The exterior surface of a coastal home is constantly exposed to salt-air and temperature extremes and tested by coastal storms. "The objective is to minimize painting, prevent water intrusion, and eliminate wood rot behind the siding, around windows, and doors." We will show how you can repair and prevent nail heads from corroding. This chapter will explain the proper technique for pressure washing your siding to prevent water intrusion and the importance of exterior surface preparation prior to painting your coastal home.

This Chapter Includes
Surface Preparation
Pressure Washing
Rusty Nail Heads
Prime, Caulk and Paint

In our discussion of exterior surfaces in Chapter Three, polymer or vinyl shakes, rigid-foam-backed vinyl siding, or composite cement siding seem to be better choices than wood. These manufactured products require less maintenance and are more durable in a coastal environment.

A coastal home, with wood siding and wood trim will require painting every three to five years, depending on coastal storms. Strong winds from nor'easters, tropical storms, and hurricanes, as well as salt spray and beach sand, will quickly diminish the life of a paint job on oceanfront and oceanview homes. Once the sand and salt have been rinsed off, with either a water hose or pressure washer, you will realize that the painted surfaces are pitted. Wind-driven sand is not covered by insurance, which is another reason to use an exterior siding product made with the color completely through the product.

Rinsing off salt film and wind-driven sand on an oceanfront home will extend the life of the paint, and the house will maintain a brighter and cleaner appearance.

Surface Preparation

A coastal painter once told me that the most important aspect of painting a coastal home was the surface preparation. He explained that the everyday coastal environment offered unique challenges, such as hot and humid summers, winter storms, wind-driven rain with salt spray, and the occasional nor'easter and hurricane.

He showed me how gaps in the siding joints can cause wood rot to wall sheathing and studs. During the planning and construction phase, the vertical siding seams should be minimized to prevent water intrusion. Even if you have a waterproof house-wrap or foam board behind the siding, always minimize the amount of siding seams and the gap size in the seams. When using wood siding, choose a siding grade with a minimum of defects and knots. Loose and even solid knots in wood can dry out and crack, allowing for water intrusion. Coastal homes will flex when being buffeted by high winds. Caulking is so important that all exterior joints, including window trim, door trim, and corner boards, need to be inspected annually. He explained the importance of using a premium grade silicone caulk that will adhere to the surface and stay flexible.

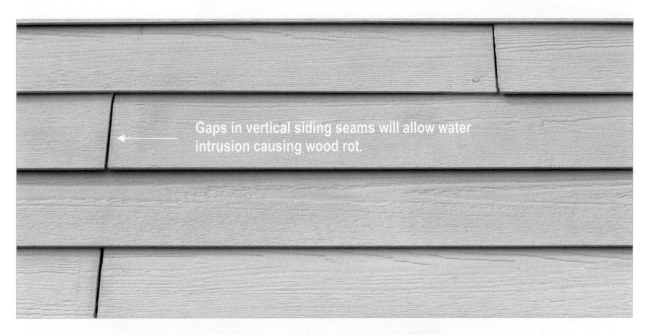

Gaps in vertical siding seams will allow water intrusion causing wood rot.

Inspect all exterior joints for cracks and gaps. Caulk with a premium paintable silicone caulk. Re-inspect annually to prevent wind-driven rain from penetrating behind the siding.

Pressure Washing

Clean the exterior surface to remove the salt film, sand, dirt, and mildew or anything that might inhibit the bond between the surface and the paint. The fastest way to clean the surface is with a pressure washer. When using a pressure washer, you must use the correct technique to prevent surface damage to the siding. Depending on the size of the pressure washer, the water pressure from the nozzle can be greater than wind-driven rain from a hurricane. Do not hold the nozzle too close to the siding. Use a fan nozzle tip. Direct the nozzle in a downward, horizontal spray. Using an vertical horizontal spray (as shown in the photo below) may result in water penetrating behind the siding, just like wind-driven rain in a nor'easter, tropical storm, or hurricane. Do not assume the contractor or handyman will use the downward, horizontal method when pressure washing your coastal home.

This vertical horizontal spray can force water behind the siding causing wood rot.

Rusty Nail Heads

The closer a coastal home is to the ocean, the more likely it is to have rusty nail heads. This is caused by the salt environment and excessive weathering that has worn away the nails protective coating (galvanized and steel-coated nails). Prior to painting the siding, the surface needs to be clean and rust free. As we have discussed, nails, fasteners, and hardware will corrode unless they are stainless steel or some other specially coated noncorrosive material. Painting over a rusty nail head will temporarily cover an ongoing problem. The rust will eventually reappear long before the house needs to be repainted. All the cost to repaint the house will be lost.

Oceanview home with corroded hot-dipped galvanized nail heads. Corrosion on a nail head can affect the structural integrity of the siding.

There are products available at your local coastal hardware, paint store, marine-supply, or home improvement store to treat, coat, convert, or dissolve rust before painting. Reference the Coastal Products Directory.

There are several options to repair and eliminate rusty nail heads:

1. For lightly corroded nails, the photos below will show how you can repair rusty nail heads. Use a stainless steel or brass hand brush or power brush to remove loose rust scale from the nail head. Choose a product from the above photo to apply to the nail head that will neutralize, convert, or dissolve the rust. Several coats may be required. This prepares the nail head for a rust-inhibitive oil primer and a finish coat of paint. **Note:** *This repair option may not be the final solution. Salt-air and weathering, particularly on oceanfront or oceanview homes, may expose the nail head, and the nail will continue to rust.*

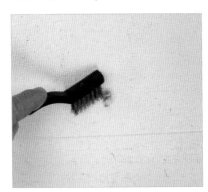

Remove loose rust scale.

Spray on rust converter, let dry.

Apply oil primer and paint.

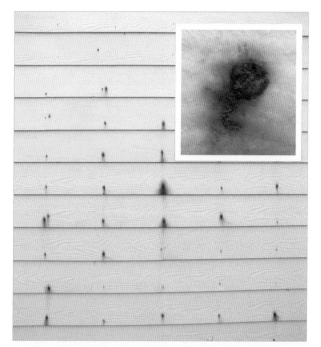
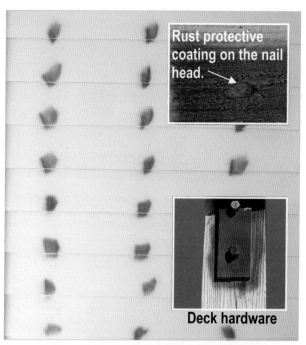

Rust protective coating on the nail head.

Deck hardware

2. The left photo shows exterior siding with corroded nail heads. Another repair option is to sand or wire-brush loose rust from the heads. (Reference the insert photo on the top right.) Apply an industrial grade, rust-inhibitive coating onto the nail heads and let dry. Then, use a rust inhibitor oil primer. Apply a finish coat of premium, severe-weather paint. Again, this repair may not be the final solution if your coastal home is oceanfront or oceanview. (Reference the insert photo on the bottom right. You can also use this repair method to treat and protect corroded deck hardware.

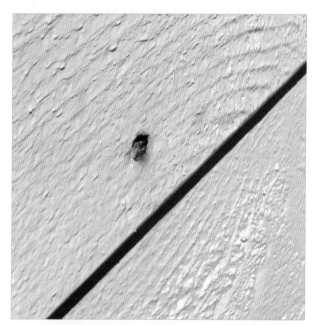

3a. A more permanent option for lightly corroded nail heads is to sand or wire-brush the rust from the nail head or apply a rust remover product to the head.

3b. Countersink the nail head just below the surface of the siding, but be careful not to counter-sink the nail too deep into the surface.

3c. Prime with a rust-inhibiting primer. Then caulk and fill depressed nail heads with a paintable, premium-silicone caulk. Drive a stainless steel nail above or below the affected area for added strength. A more labor-intensive, permanent solution than option one or two. A lesson learned...

4. There is one other permanent solution to eliminating rusty nail heads. If all of the siding nails are heavily corroded and deteriorated, remove the siding and rusty nails. Reinstall the same type of siding or a high-wind-rated manufactured siding product with the paint color completely through the product. Use 316 stainless steel siding nails or the manufacturer's approved fasteners. This option means no more painting or rusty nails.

Prime Coat

Wood will absorb moisture. It is very important in a coastal area to prime and seal the front, back, sides, and ends of wood siding and trim boards to keep out moisture. This includes corner boards, soffits, fascia boards, and window and door trim. **Note:** *When installing manufactured siding and trim, you may find that some products come from the factory already primed on an all six sides. Be sure to verify before installing.*

Fiber-cement trim boards that have all the advantages of wood without any of wood's limitations. They have been primed at the factory on all six sides. The trim is impact and termite resistant. This product can be installed with traditional methods and tools. (*Photo courtesy of Plycem, Inc.*) Reference the Coastal Products Directory pg.154 chapter three.

Caulk

Prior to repainting your coastal home, caulk and seal all trim boards to prevent moisture intrusion and wood rot. Use premium grade, exterior-paintable caulking that will stay flexible in extreme weather conditions. Coastal homes are often buffeted by high winds and wind-driven rain. The time and money you spend on this task will pay dividends. The bottom and right photos show caulk being applied to door, window, and corner trim. **Note:** *Caulked joints should be inspected annually and re-caulk if necessary to prevent water intrusion.*

Paint

When choosing a paint, consult your coastal paint dealer, coastal hardware, or home improvement store for information on the best exterior paint for your application. Review the latest consumer report ratings for exterior paint. Make sure the rating addresses severe weather conditions.

Here's a final word on surface preparation: Never paint over damp or wet wood. Inspect carefully for soft spots and wood rot. Find where the moisture originated, and repair and replace immediately before it causes a more costly repair.

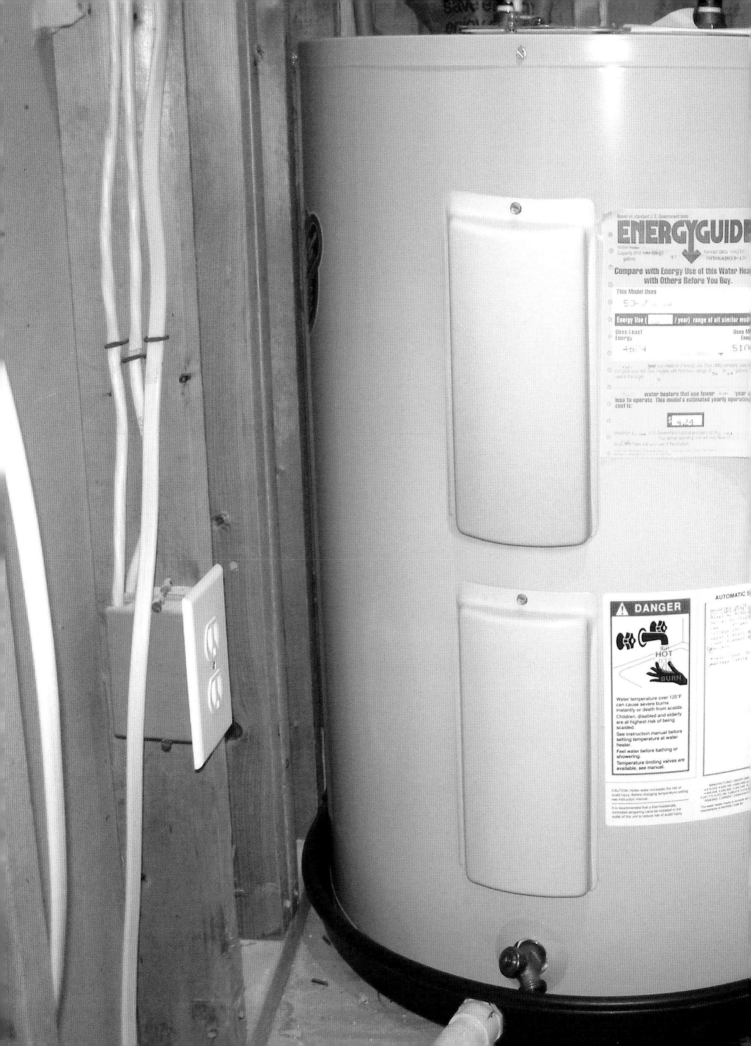

ENERGYGUIDE

Compare with Energy Use of this Water Heater
with Others Before You Buy.

This Model Uses

Energy Use (/ year) range of all similar models

Uses Least
Energy

Uses Most
Energy

water heaters that use fewer / year
less to operate. This model's estimated yearly operating
cost is:

⚠ DANGER

HOT
BURN

Water temperature over 125°F
can cause severe burns
instantly or death from scalds.
Children, disabled and elderly
are at highest risk of being
scalded.
See instruction manual before
setting temperature at water
heater.
Feel water before bathing or
showering.
Temperature limiting valves are
available, see manual.

AUTOMATIC S

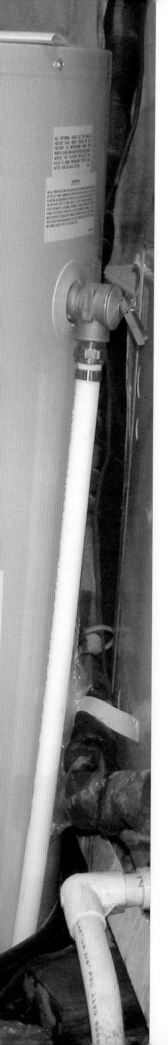

8

Water Heaters

I *n coastal areas, the placement of a water heater is very*
important. Water heaters need to be monitored closely for
corrosion.

Most homes have at least one hot-water heater. After years
of continual use, a water heater will let you know when it is time to
be replaced. It will either leak or the water will suddenly become
cold. In most regions of the country, the placement of a hot-water
heater inside your home has minimal impact on the life expectancy
of the unit. In a coastal home, however, the location and placement
of the hot-water heater will contribute greatly to its life expectancy.
When installing a hot-water heater, considering some important
environmental factors will save you time, money, and frustration.

This chapter will address exterior corrosion, sediment build-
up, and flushing requirements. Also, we will discuss how water
softeners and whole-house sediment filters can extend the life of
a hot-water heater and plumbing fixtures.

This Chapter Includes
Sediment Build-Up
Flushing Water Heaters
Installation and Monitoring
Water Softeners and Filters

In a perfect world, you would never give a second thought to your water heater—certainly not while you are standing under a refreshingly hot shower. In fact, once purchased and installed, our water heaters are generally "out of sight, out of mind." However, when water suddenly goes cold, we begin to think about the hot-water heater.

We arrive for a long, relaxing weekend at our coastal home to find the ceiling dripping water, the carpet soaked, and the ground floor flooded. We quickly become aware that our hot-water heater is the single most important appliance in our house—the one appliance that can cause serious damage. Sediment and corrosion build-up inside the tank are often the cause of the water heater leaking. There can be an additional issue in a coastal environment: corrosion can build-up on the outside of the tank, causing the water heater to leak.

Sediment Build-Up

Sediment exists in almost every tank-style water heater. Some coastal areas are noted for their hard water. Hard water can result in mineral and rust build-up in the bottom of the tank. Mineral scale can shorten the life of the heating elements inside an electric water heater. When sediment scale builds up, you can hear popping noises or other sounds coming from the tank. This can significantly affect your water heater's performance and shorten the life of the tank. In a gas water heater, mineral scale can create a buffer between the bottom of the tank that is heated by the burner and the water itself. The heater will not operate as efficiently, and you may hear a strange rumbling noise.

Sediments will accumulate in the bottom of a water heater below the drain valve. Coastal homeowners should remove sediments from inside their water heaters periodically to minimize build-up. **Note:** *A professional plumber is recommend to perform the following procedure.* Make sure the water heater has been turned off and drained. Secure a wet/dry shop vacuum. Seal off the end of the vacuum hose with duct tape. Wrap several times to completely seal off the hose end. Cut a small diameter hole in the center of the duct tape. Secure a ½"or ¾"diameter clear plastic,

flexible tubing, approximately 4' long. Slowly insert one end of the clear plastic tubing through the hole in the duct tape. Push the plastic tubing approximately 1' inside the vacuum hose. Make sure there is a tight seal around the plastic tubing and the duct tape. If necessary, wrap duct tape around the tube-to-hose connection several times. Remove the bottom heating element from the water heater. Insert the other end of the flexible plastic tubing in the water heater. Turn on the shop vacuum to see mineral scale and rust being removed through the clear plastic tubing. When completed, this would be a good opportunity to reinstall new heating elements.

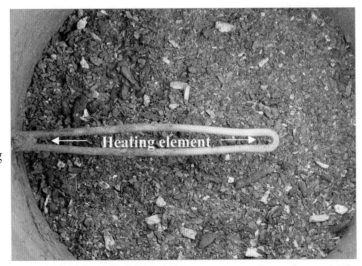

Mineral scale and rust build-up in the bottom of a coastal water heater. Sediment can affect the performance and life expectancy of the water heater.

Flushing Hot Water Heaters

Flushing a water heater is a maintenance procedure that is not very difficult. You need a garden hose and a place to drain the water. The procedure generally involves the following. If your water heater is gas, set the gas valve to "pilot" to prevent the burners from coming on when flushing. If your water heater is electric make sure you turn off the circuit breaker. With an electric water heater, if the water level drops below the heating elements and the thermostat turns the elements on, the heating elements can burn out. Connect the garden hose to the drain valve at the bottom of the water heater. The other end of the garden hose should be placed in a bath tub or closest low-point drain. Close the cold water inlet valve on top of the heater. Carefully open the pressure relief valve at the top of the heater by lifting the lever. Leave the valve open. Turn on the

drain valve allowing the water to flow out through the garden hose. Be careful, the water will be very hot. If sediments are clogging the drain valve, close the pressure relief valve and turn the cold water inlet valve back on to swirl the water around to flush the sediments out. When clear water is running through the garden hose the tank is cleaned. **Note:** *If the drain valve remains clogged, refer to the sediment build-up procedure on the previous page.* Disconnect the water hose and close the bottom drain valve. Close the pressure relief valve by pushing down on the lever. Open a hot water faucet in your home and let the water run until it runs smoothly, eliminating all noisy air pockets or air bubbles in the line.

Top photo shows a garden hose connected to a hot-water heater drain valve.

Turn the circuit breaker back on. If you have a gas water heater re-light the pilot light if necessary. **Note:** *Refer to your owners manual for specific instructions on how to flush your model and style water heater. Always use caution when flushing a water heater, there is a danger of being scalded. If you are not sure, call a professional plumber Also, you can go online and search for," how to flush a water heater."* Water heater manufactures recommend flushing periodically

to minimize corrosion and some sediment build-up. How often depends upon the water quality in your area. Coastal areas with a high mineral content will have to be flushed more often.

Left photo shows the garden hose draining into a bathtub, or find the closest low-point drain. When clear water is running through the garden hose the tank is cleaned.

Installation and Monitoring

Whether you are newly constructing or renovating a coastal home, never install a water heater inside your home in an unconditioned air space where salt air and moisture may be in the environment. The tank and fittings will corrode on the outside, causing it to leak. Never install a water heater in an attic space. The attic space in a coastal home can be very corrosive due to air circulating through the soffit vents and gable ends.

The philosophy "out of sight, out of mind" can lead to disaster. Remember water runs downhill. Periodically, inspect your water heater for exterior rust. Replace immediately if there is evidence of excessive corrosion on the outside. Reference the Coastal Products Directory.

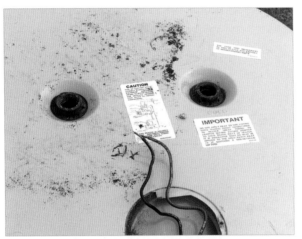

Two corroded fittings (cold-water inlet and hot-water outlet) on the top surface of a hot-water heater. Corrosion on the exterior fittings will eventually cause a water heater to leak.
Note: *This water heater was removed from a coastal home. It was installed in an unconditioned air space.*

If the bottom surface of a water heater is corroded, it's likely the interior water tank is also corroded. If a water heater has exterior corrosion, it needs to be replaced before it leaks and causes a much larger problem.

High-efficiency designed *Marathon* series hot-water heater that won't corrode, with a blow molded, polybutene tank, impervious to rust and corrosion. Multiple layers of filament-wound fiberglass gives the tank unmatched strength. A tough, molded-polyethylene outer shell resists dents and scratches. The bowl-shaped bottom allows complete sediment draining when flushing. Polyurethane envirofoam insulation helps reduce energy consumption. (*Photo courtesy of Rheem water heaters.*) Reference the Coastal Products Directory.

Water Softeners and Filters

To prevent sediment and scale build-up, install a water softener to reduce the hardness of the water. Install a whole-house sediment filter on the incoming cold-water line to remove unwanted sand and sediment particles. Purchase a water softener that won't corrode and is impervious to rust and corrosion. Reference the Coastal Products Directory.

In-line whole-house sediment filter. A filter is recommended to reduce sediment build-up inside water heaters. **Note:** *Depending on your water usage, and the amount of sediments in the water, a replacement filter may need to be installed periodically to maintain adequate water pressure. A lesson learned...*

Water softeners will reduce hard-water build-up inside your water heater and in both kitchen and bath fixtures.

Water heaters are often installed inside a plastic drain pan. For additional protection install a portable moisture alarm inside the drain pan. The alarm will sound if any moisture is detected in the pan. The moisture alarm is inexpensive and can be purchased at a coastal hardware or home improvement store. Do not rely solely on the drain pan. Water may leak faster from a corroded water heater than it will drain from the pan. In addition, the drain line from the pan might be clogged. **Note:** *Local building codes will govern the installation of water heaters.*

A water alarm inside a plastic drain pan. Both products will prevent or minimize water damage from a leaking hot-water heater.

9

Coastal Roofs

A coastal roof should do more than just beautify your home. The roof system should be designed and installed to withstand high winds and the coastal environment. Tropical storms, hurricanes and even winter storms, can create serious damage to roof coverings. When roofing materials fail and blow-off, water damage and high winds can lead to dangerous structural damage.

As one of my lessons learned, I have decided there are two types of roofs on coastal homes, roofs that require frequent, costly, and frustrating repairs caused by high winds from coastal storms and wind-rated roof systems designed and tested for coastal areas. A quality roof system for a coastal home is a substantial investment. As we have already discussed in Chapter Two, Doors and Windows, uninformed choices will cost thousands of dollars in repairs, repeat maintenance and replacement cost.

This chapter will give you low-maintenance options when choosing a roof system. You will be introduced to different types of wind-rated roof systems that are designed for the coastal environment.

This Chapter Includes
Metal Roofing Panels
Asphalt Shingles
Metal or Composite Shingles
Roof Repairs
Flashing

Years ago, right after I built a coastal home, I was watching the news, and I saw a report on a gulf coast town that had just experienced a category-one hurricane. The broadcast included footage of homeowners installing blue tarps for temporary protection. At that moment, I realized how important the proper roofing material was in a coastal environment. The category-one hurricane left more shingles scattered on the streets and yards than were left on the roofs. With nor'easters, tropical storms, and hurricane-force winds causing a threat to your coastal home, your choice of roof is a very important decision.

The increase in insurance deductibles has accelerated in recent years. The out-of-pocket expenses have increased. Some policies state that replacement can only be "like kind" quality, and that may leave you with a roof repair that may not match exactly instead of a complete roof replacement.

It only takes a nor'easter or a summer storm to damage a roof that is not designed for a coastal environment. In addition, having to get a roofing contractor to make repairs several times a year can be frustrating and expensive.

Metal Roofing Panels

To ensure your metal roof will withstand the coastal elements, salt air, and high winds, consider a roof system that has a high wind rating, with a noncorrosive warranty. The roof panels may be manufactured of stainless steel or 100 percent aluminum with a KYNAR paint coating. They should be installed with noncorrosive hidden fasteners. There are some metal roof systems designed and installed with hundreds of self-taping screw heads exposed to the coastal elements. Screw heads that will corrode and deteriorate very quickly if not designed for the salt air and salt spray environment.

Not all metal roof systems are manufactured with a noncorrosive warranty and wind rating. If your coastal home is exposed to the salt-air, salt spray, and high winds, the material construction, fasteners, and installation warranty is very important.

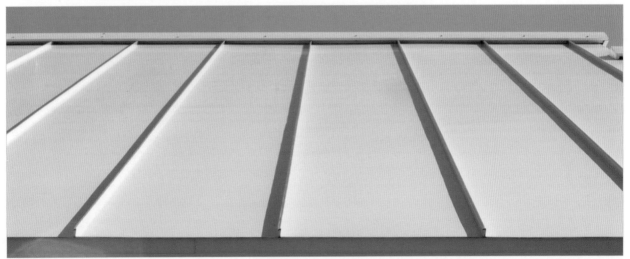

This standing seam, wind-rated aluminum roof has a KYNAR paint coating, design and installed with hidden fasteners for a clean design, that won't corrode in a salt-air environment.

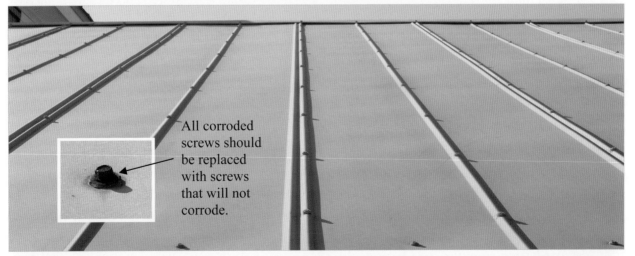

All corroded screws should be replaced with screws that will not corrode.

The above metal roof panels are corrosion resistant. Some of the self-taping screws are not. The enlarged insert photo, shows a screw head that has already corroded. Corroded screw heads can affect the structural integrity of the entire roof system. If fasteners are exposed to the salt-air environment, make sure they are made of noncorrosive material.

Asphalt Shingles

Another good choice is asphalt shingles with extra-wide adhesive bands for maximum hold-down strength. Choose an asphalt shingle that is wind rated and tested by Underwriters Laboratories. Wind-rated shingles are rated in three classes.

1. Class D: Wind speeds up to 90 miles per hour
2. Class G: Wind speeds up to 120 miles per hour
3. Class H: Wind speeds up to 150 miles per hour

Shingles rated in a wind-resistance class will need to be installed according to coastal building codes and manufacturer's specifications. **Note:** *Contact your local building inspections department for the wind-speed zone in your coastal area.*

Asphalt-shingle roofs that are designed for the coastal environment. The 110-mile-per-hour wind rated *Hatteras* shingles installed with a high-performance starter shingle. Specifically for use with Hatteras shingles, the dual sealant strips, located at the bottom edge to resist blow-off. **Note***: Shingles should be installed according to coastal building code requirements and manufacturer's installation instructions. (Both photos are courtesy of Certain Teed Inc*.) Reference the Coastal Products Directory.

Metal or Composite Shingles

Metal or composite shingles have the beauty of wood shake, slate, or tile shingles. These roofs are a premium choice, with little or no maintenance. Install with hidden fasteners, according to the manufacturer's specifications, to achieve a maximum wind resistance of 80 to 160 miles per hour, depending on the product.

A final note: The roof begins with the underlayment. When installing a new roof or re-roofing an existing roof, take this opportunity to use a peel-and-seal flashing tape to cover all sheathing joints. For problem areas, use ice and water shield, (a rubberized material that comes in a roll just like felt paper.) A secondary moisture barrier, flashing tape, ice and water shield products will maximize your roofs protection from wind-driven rain. As for the underlayment, install 30-pound asphalt-saturated felt, secured with galvanized roofing nails. **Note:** *Roofing manufacturer's may recommend or specify a particular underlayment for their roof system.* Reference the Coastal Products Directory for companies that provide roofing products designed for coastal areas.

The left photo is a stone coated metal roof, manufactured by Gerard Metal Roofing System. Timberwood Canyon shake.

The bottom photo is a stone coated metal roof also manufactured by Gerard Metal Roofing System. Cypress Barrel Vault.
Both roofs are installed with hidden fasteners and are designed for a high wind rating. (*Photos courtesy of Metals USA Roofing.*) Reference the Coastal Products Directory.

Roof Repairs

Caulk loose shingle tabs down with roofing cement to increase holding strength.

Areas of concern in maintaining a roof are the vent pipes, chimneys, eaves, valleys, dormers and ridge caps. Inspect these areas annually to identify and repair any potential problems. Have a professional roofing contractor inspect your roof for any loose shingle tabs. Apply roofing cement under the tab for additional holding strength. This practice can save you money and aggravation over time. A lesson learned…

Flashing

Roof flashing is an important aspect of any roof system. Flashing a coastal roof properly can prevent costly water damage. At a minimum, coastal roof flashing needs to be corrosion resistant and meet the minimum thickness requirements. The closer your home is to the coast, especially oceanfront, oceanview, or soundfront, copper, stainless steel, and vinyl flashing becomes the better choices. A coastal roofing contractor or building inspector can give advice on the preferable roof flashing material for your location. **Note:** *Local building codes will govern the installation process of a coastal roof to maximize water and wind resistance.*

 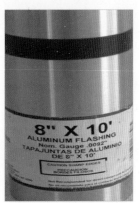  

Copper roof flashing   Aluminum roof flashing   Galvanized roof flashing   Vinyl roof flashing

Lint build-up on this dryer-vent cap prevents the flapper-valve from shutting completely, allowing for water intrusion. Excess lint inside the duct can also be a safety hazard.

The louvers on this vent cap are stuck in the open position, allowing for wind-driven rain to enter the house.

10

Preventive Maintenance

*D*eteriorated or damaged exterior wall and roof-vent caps in a coastal environment is a major cause of water intrusion. They should be repaired or replaced immediately.

To minimize repeat maintenance, inspect for damaged, deteriorated, or corroded wall caps. Moisture intrusion caused by wind-driven rain can get behind the wall. The moisture can lead to wood rot in the sheathing and wall studs.

In this chapter, paying close attention to details will prove to be invaluable in adapting your home to the coastal environment. To save time and money, we will explain how small problems can lead to more expensive problems.

This Chapter Includes
Exterior Wall and Roof Caps
Exterior Faucets
Exterior Wall Penetrations
Concrete Driveways
Mechanical Equipment
Appliance Supply Lines
Shower Heads
Window Treatments

Maintaining the beauty and integrity of any coastal home, regardless of size or location, is an ongoing project. There is always something that needs to be repaired to maintain property values and prevent further deterioration. Some of these tasks are aesthetic, and some, if they are not addressed properly, can result in a much larger and more expensive problem.

In this context, the old saying, "a stitch in time saves nine" is certainly appropriate. Routine preventative maintenance will save you time, aggravation, and money, especially in coastal regions where the salt-air environment can cause corrosion and metal fatigue. Wind-driven rain can lead to wood rot, mold, mildew, and termite infestation.

Exterior Wall and Roof Caps

Most of us never give any thought to vents, passageways, and ducts through which gases, smoke, and heat are removed from the house. Direct-vent gas fireplaces require fresh air to be vented in, while fumes and gases are vented out of the house. When vent ducts are installed, they are often routed to an exterior wall or roof area. When termination vent caps are originally installed, local building codes will govern the installation. Vent caps are essential; they protect a coastal home from wind-driven rain, wood rot, birds, and pests, and they keep the coastal environment outside. Years ago as an uninformed homeowner, I was told by a coastal framing carpenter that a small problem can easily turn into a larger problem in a coastal area.

The integrity of the wall and roof caps must be maintained to allow for the proper functioning of appliances and the health and well-being of everyone in the home. As you walk around the exterior of your home, inspect the various vent caps to see if they are damaged or corroded. Inspect the caulking, and recaulk if needed. In a coastal area, if vent caps have been left damaged, hidden problems may have developed. Remove the vent cap and look for other damage, including wood rot. Repair and replace all wood rot immediately. Reinstall new, non-corroding plastic or corrosive resistant metal vent caps with stainless steel screws. Caulk and seal around the new wall or roof cap to prevent water intrusion caused by wind-driven rain. Investigate the availability of a corrosive-resistant or non-corroding wall and roof caps at your local hardware or home improvement store. *Reference the Coastal Products Directory.*

A corroded metal vent cap, like the one shown in the bottom left photo, may not function as it should. It may also lead to water intrusion behind the exterior wall or beneath the roof. This could cause larger and more expensive problems, including wood rot, if not replaced in a timely manor.

Replace with a stainless steel or aluminum vent cap as shown in the bottom right photo. They will not bleed rust stains on the siding. Use stainless steel screws when installing stainless or aluminum exterior vent caps.

Range Vent Caps

A range-vent cap terminates the duct that carries smoke and cooking odors from the range. The vent cap in the photo is corroded. Remove and replace with a vent cap that is corrosive resistant. Reference the Coastal Products Directory for stainless steel or aluminum vent caps designed for wall and roof installation. Visit your local coastal hardware or home improvement store to locate and install a vent cap that will not corrode and bleed rust on your coastal home.

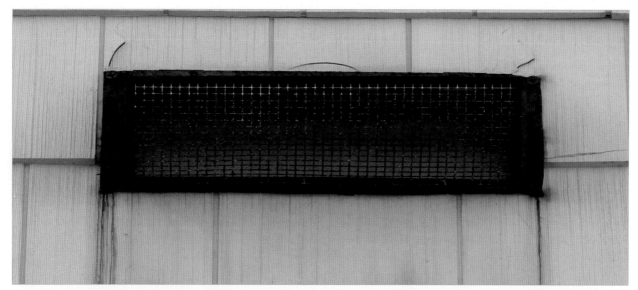

A corroded wall-vent cap with plated screws has damaged and discolored the exterior siding with rust stains. A corroded vent cap may contribute to moisture intrusion behind the siding.

Plastic vent caps will not corrode, but they will deteriorate as the photo shows. Vent caps need to be inspected periodically for wind damage and replaced. **Right photo shows** a stainless steel wall vent cap with a spring damper, weather seal, wind guard, bird screen, and stainless steel screws. *Stainless steel vent caps are corrosive resistant.*

Dryer-Vent Caps

Dryer-vent caps come in several styles. They can be a major source of water intrusion. They terminate the duct that allows hot air from the dryer to be vented outside. These termination caps are often available in plastic, which will not corrode. However, in hot, humid climates and the salt-air environment, the plastic may dry out, become brittle, and deteriorate. High winds and rain can also damage a vent cap or force a vent cap damper or louvers to open. Remove and replace the cap at the first sign of damage or deterioration to prevent water damage behind the exterior wall or roof. Plastic vent caps can be purchase at a coastal hardware or home improvement store or reference the Coastal Products Directory for dryer-vent caps.

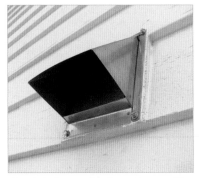

A stainless steel-vent cap with spring damper, weather seal, wind guard, and stainless steel screws.

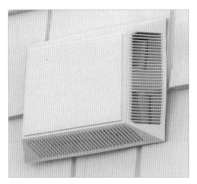

This plastic-vent cap does not have moving parts, such as louvers or a damper.

A plastic-vent cap with an exterior bird screen and a interior damper.

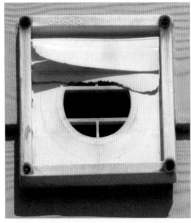

Plastic louvers can become brittle in the sun and deteriorate, leaving the opening exposed to the coastal elements. The plated screws are corroded. Install a new wall-vent cap with stainless steel screws.

These louvers are stuck in the open position. This allows for wind-driven rain to penetrate the opening, damaging sheathing and wall studs. High winds and wind-driven rain in a coastal region can damage exterior vent caps. **Note**: *Painting exterior Vents can caused the louvers not to open and closed properly.*

The plastic damper is missing on this hooded vent cap. This also allows for wind-driven rain and small insects and birds to enter the dryer duct. Small rodents can cause major damage inside your home.

Fireplace Vent Caps

Direct-vent fireplaces exhaust hot fumes and intake fresh air through an inner-core and outer-duct design also called a double-wall duct. Corrosion could not only limit their effectiveness but also present a safety hazard. If the fasteners are corroded, the vent caps may not hold a firm seal to the exterior siding or roof. This may allow for water intrusion and further deterioration of untreated wood. Contact the manufacturer concerning your model fireplace to research the possibility of a non-corroding, or corrosive resistant direct-vent termination cap. Reference the Coastal Products Directory for stainless steel vent caps designed for walls and roofs.

Corroded wall-vent caps that can be a source for water intrusion behind the exterior siding and may inhibit the performance of the fireplace.

A non-corroding direct-vent fireplace wall cap.

Corrosive-resistant stainless steel direct-vent fireplace wall cap.

Exterior Faucets (Hose Bibs, Sill Cocks)

A water hose is a convenient tool that can be used to rinse off exterior surfaces. It is essential for maintaining a coastal home. You want to be sure your faucets (hose bibs) are always securely fastened to the house. Coastal homes are often multi-level, with each level having a deck and a hose bib. Take a moment to inspect each of your exterior faucets, and look for a gap or open space between the hose bibs and the exterior wall. Moisture or wind-driven rain can pass through the gap to saturate the siding, wall sheathing, and studs. This is one area where a small problem can lead to a much larger problem if not addressed immediately. A lesson learned... When installing a water-hose hanger, make sure it is attached to the house with stainless steel screws. Choose a non-corroding or plastic water-hose hanger that won't deteriorate or bleed rust onto your siding.

Notice the large gap between the hose bib and the wall and the corroded screws. Repair or replace to prevent water damage behind the exterior siding.

A stainless steel water-hose hanger secured with stainless steel screws will not rust or dry out and crack as most metal or plastic water hose-hangers will.

The hose bib to the left is secured with stainless steel screws. It's fitted tightly to the wall, and it has been caulked with a premium exterior silicone caulk to prevent water intrusion.

Exterior Wall Penetrations

Wall penetrations on a coastal home should always be avoided to minimize water intrusion caused by wind-driven rain. If a hole is required, keep the hole diameter to a minimum.

 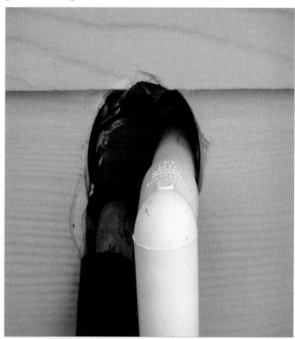

In each of the photos the hole in the exterior wall is much larger than the copper tubing or PVC pipe. This will lead to heating and cooling loss, water intrusion, pests, and rodents.

 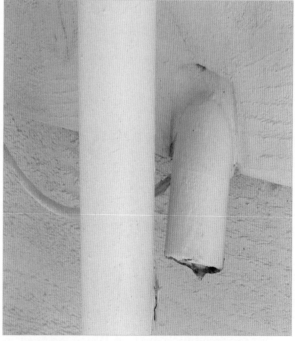

The hole should be filled with spray-foam insulation and a paintable, premium exterior silicone caulk. Corrosive resistant metal flashing can be cut, form-fitted, and caulked in place around the penetration.

Concrete Driveways

Most homes in coastal areas are built on sand. Sand, more than most other soils, is susceptible to slight shifts. This can sometimes result in cracks appearing in concrete driveways. Like any crack, these will only become bigger and will need to be repaired to limit the damage that can occur from freezing, thaw cycles, and moisture intrusion.

A driveway with several cracks. While these hairline cracks look small and inconsequential, they allow moisture to enter and cause more damage.

The appropriate repair method. Widen the crack in a controlled manner and fill with an approved-expandable concrete repair product supplied by your coastal hardware or home-improvement store.

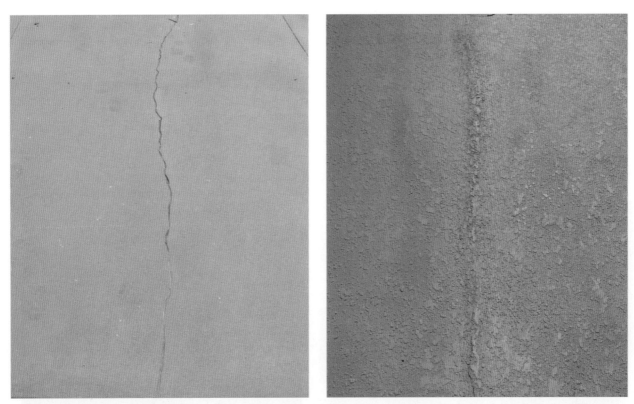

Left photo shows a repaired crack in a concrete driveway. **The right photo shows** a repaired crack in a concrete driveway, and the driveway has been restored by resurfacing with a decorative overlay product made specifically for restoring concrete surfaces. This product can help conceal cracks and blemishes and give, the appearance of an upgraded surface finish. Annual maintenance may be required.

With sufficient control joints, soil compaction, including a rebar mat, and/ or welded wire mesh, for reinforcement, your driveway can remain crack-free and looking good for years. **Note:** *Local building codes will govern the installation of driveways.*

Mechanical Equipment

As discussed in a previous chapter, there are various ways to extend the life of outside equipment in a coastal environment. In recent years, inground swimming pools have become very popular with coastal homeowners and their guests. The initial cost of the mechanical equipment can be very expensive.

Recirculation pumps, heaters, control cabinets, and electronics can get expensive to maintain or replace. The closer you live to the coast, the more protection the equipment requires. Salt air, salt spray, wind-driven debris, and sand can reduce the life of all mechanical equipment.

Swimming pool recirculation equipment exposed to the salt-air environment will corrode.

At a minimum, build a wall around the equipment for protection. For maximum protection, build a total enclosure. Have your equipment serviced annually to maintain peak performance.

Appliance Supply Lines

Certain appliances require water-supply lines. A washing machine uses a hot-and cold-water supply line, usually a reinforced rubber line. An ice maker will use a cold-water supply line usually plastic tubing. After the water lines are installed, we never give any thought to them. It is only when you walk-in and realize you have a leak and the house has water damage that you think about the water lines. You rush to call a plumber, and the only advice he can offer is that you should have upgraded to stainless steel braided water lines. The stainless steel supply lines will not deteriorate and are more resistant to cold, freezing weather. Coastal homes are not always occupied during the winter months. When the heat is turned off and the house has not been winterized, the small, plastic ice-maker line may freeze and burst. (Winterizing is discussed in chapter 11.) The water will continue to run until someone turns it off. Stainless steel braided water-supply lines are the best value to protect your coastal home from water damage. Appliance supply lines can be purchased at a coastal hardware or home-improvement stores.

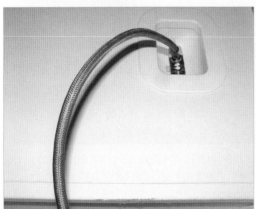

Make sure the water supply lines to all your appliances are stainless steel braided. **The top photo** shows the hot-and cold -water lines on a washing machine being changed from reinforced rubber line to a stainless steel braided line.
The left photo shows an ice-maker supply line behind the refrigerator, that has been changed from plastic tubing to a stainless steel braided line. **Note:** *As rubber and plastic ages it begins to deteriorate .*

Shower Heads

Coastal homes often require a water softener and an inline, whole-house sediment filter. If a water softener has not been installed, or an installed water softener is not functioning properly, calcium and lime can build up on faucets and shower heads. Calcium, lime, and sediments will impede the flow of water. Remove the shower head and clean out the sediments from the wire strainer. Next, remove the calcium deposits with a cleaner approved for removing calcium and lime deposits.

A shower head with calcium build-up that can restrict water flow.

A typical wire strainer located in most faucet and shower heads. Remove sediment and clean out periodically to increase water flow. Install an inline, whole-house sediment filter to reduce build-up. **Note:** *See chapter eight, page 87.*

Calcium can be removed with an approved cleaner. Always follow directions on the product label.

Approved cleaners to remove calcium and hard-water deposits. Always read the label before applying to any surface.

Window Treatments

When choosing window treatments, most homeowners consider style, pricing, and function. Coastal homeowners must also consider material construction. The closer your home is to the coast, the more corrosion becomes an issue. For example, installing a window blind with a top and bottom rail made from metal that corrodes will only detract from the beauty of your home. Corrosion from the salt-air will occur when the windows are left open to catch the summer breeze. Window treatments can be very expensive, so you want to make the best decision the first time. Search for blinds with a top and bottom rail that will not corrode.

The insert photos shows a top and bottom rail on a window blind that has corroded in a salt-air environment. The blinds were removed from a coastal home and replaced with the blinds below.

Install blinds made of materials that will not corrode, especially the top and bottom rails. Window treatments are available in wood, faux wood (PVC), aluminum, and fabrics. These will give you lasting beauty and performance. A lesson learned...

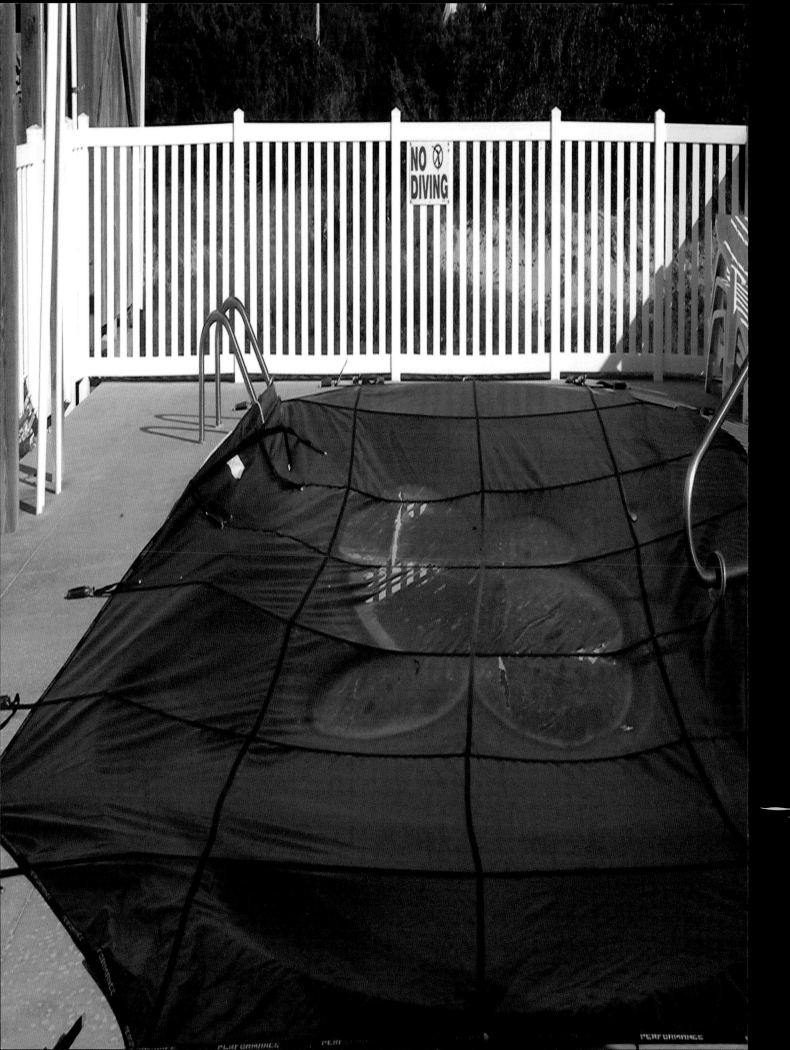

11

Winterizing Coastal Homes

After you have winterized your pool, it is a good idea to install a pool cover for winter storm protection to prevent wind-driven sand and debris from entering the pool.

If your coastal home is used only during the warm summer months, you will need to winterize.

This chapter will show how you can prepare your home for a partial or complete winterization and be confident your home will be ready to use the following summer. Also included are security tips for monitoring and protecting your home while you are away.

This Chapter Includes

Indoor Cleaning
Partial Winterization
Complete Winterization
Winterizing Hot Tubs and Swimming Pools
Home Security
Winterizing Checklist

There are coastal homes that are occupied year-round. Other homes are used either by owners or by vacation guests only during the warm summer months. When preparing your home for winterizing, there are a number of specific areas that you need to address. The one phone call you don't want to get is from someone informing you that a pipe has frozen or burst in your home.

Knowing your home will be in great shape to welcome you back the following summer will save you time, money, and aggravation. While you are taking advantage of the last days of summer, make sure you plan ahead for what is required to winterize your coastal home. Even if you have professional personnel scheduled to do most of the work, there are some tasks that you may want to do yourself.

Indoor Cleaning

To avoid a musty smell when you return, make sure all your linens are cleaned, dried, and packed away in plastic bins. Also, make sure the house has been thoroughly cleaned, including the carpet and upholstery. Clean out all open food boxes in the cabinets, and remove the food in the refrigerator. Take out the trash. Place an open box of baking soda in the refrigerator to absorb any residual odors. You can place additional odor absorbers in the closets to keep them smelling fresh.

Clean carpet, upholstery, and rugs to minimize musty odors during the off season. Also, install odor absorbents in the closets and the refrigerator.

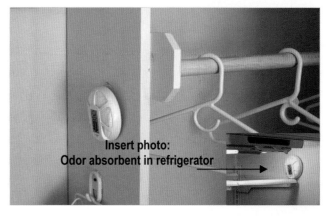

Insert photo:
Odor absorbent in refrigerator

Partial Winterization

If your coastal home is in a location where the winters are mild and the temperature seldom drops below freezing, keep your central heat set on the lowest temperature setting, normally 40 or 50 degrees Fahrenheit. This will prevent your inside water lines, ice-maker lines, and toilets from freezing. The heat will reduce the humidity inside the house and help prevent mold and mildew.

If you have a direct-vent fireplace, leave the pilot light burning. The heat from the pilot light will prevent humidity and salt moisture from corroding the duct and the enclosed firebox. Salt moisture will also damage the ignition system inside the firebox, resulting in expensive repairs. Set up automatic delivery to monitor your gas supply during the winter months. For a wood-burning fireplace that will not be used, close the flue and cap the chimney to keep birds and pests out. Remove and store deck chairs, tables, and the grill to keep them protected from winter storms.

Turn off non-essential circuit breakers in the electrical panel box.

Leave the pilot light burning to dry out salt-moisture on the inside of the duct and enclosed firebox. Salt-moisture will corrode the exhaust duct and firebox. A lesson learned...

113

Complete Winterization

If your coastal home is located in an area where the temperature drops below freezing and you decide to turn your central heating system off, you may need a professional to fully drain and winterize all plumbing. Begin by shutting off the main water supply coming into the house. Open and leave on all faucets and exterior hose bibs to allow water to drain, including water lines and toilets. Flush the toilets, and then pour nontoxic antifreeze in the tank and the bowl. Also, add antifreeze to all shower, tub, and sink drains. **Note:** *Nontoxic antifreeze is available at most marine-and RV-supply stores.*

Have your plumber drain your hot-water heater, water softener, ice maker, washing machine, and dishwasher lines. Also, drain all exterior showers, sinks, and sprinkler systems. If you decide to turn off your pilot light on the direct-vent fireplace during the winter months, consider installing a protective cap over the outside vent. This will help prevent salt-air and moisture from entering the duct and firebox. Call your gas company to turn off the gas supply coming into the house. Reference the Coastal Products Directory.

A non-toxic anti-freeze being poured into a sink, a bath tub, a toilet tank and bowl to prevent freezing.

Winterizing Hot Tubs and Swimming Pools

Closing down your hot tub or swimming pool for the winter requires a detailed procedure to ensure that all water has been removed. Most damage that occurs to hot tubs and pools is caused by improper winterization. Procedures may vary depending on the pool or spa. There are different winterizing procedures for both in-ground and above-ground pools. The location or climate condition will also determine how pools and hot tubs should be winterized. Trace amounts of water in the water supply or drain lines will freeze and may cause serious damage. Spas and pools are a major investment. If you are hesitant to perform this service, ask your local pool or spa company, or your property management company, to provide this service. If you decide to do it yourself, visit **www.poolandspa.com** for a list of procedures to complete this process.

Winterizing your hot tub and pool should be performed by qualified personnel. It requires that all trace amounts of water be removed. This can be achieved by draining the lines in addition to using a wet-dry vac.

Home Security

Some coastal areas offer a service that will have someone check your property on a weekly or monthly schedule. This is a great service if you do not have someone you can call to check on your property. The investment of having some form of security check is money well spent. Call the police department and inform them that you are leaving for the winter, and the house will be unoccupied. Leave them your contact information.

Ensure your alarm system is working, and activate it upon leaving the property.

If your car is packed and you are ready to say good-bye to your coastal home for the season, remember to lock your windows and close your blinds. Install or engage your hurricane shutter systems for winter storm protection and added security. Activate your security system, if you have one. Lock and deadbolt your doors. Install tape over the keyhole cylinder to prevent salt air and moisture from entering the lockset. Head home for the winter, knowing your coastal home will be in great shape and your key will unlock the door to welcome you back next season.

Hurricane shutters add value and an added layer of security during the off season. Photo courtesy of Alutech United. Reference the Coastal Products Directory.

Place tape over the keyhole, and press on firmly for a tight seal. The tape will prevent salt-air and salt-moisture from entering the lock. This will prevent corrosion from damaging the internal pins. Your key will unlock the door when you return next season.

CHECKLIST FOR WINTERIZING YOUR COASTAL HOME

Complete winterization will include all line items.
Partial winterization is denoted with a asterisk.*

	Partial	Complete

- Call an HVAC contractor to service the heating and cooling system.* _____ _____
- Have a qualified plumber to shut off and drain the main water supply. _____ _____
- Fully drain the refrigerator water line, dishwasher, washing machine, toilets, hot-water heater, showers, water softener, and outside faucets. _____ _____
- Have qualified personnel winterize your pool and/or hot tub spa. _____ _____
- Leave the pilot light on the direct-vent fireplace to prevent corrosion.* _____ _____
- Set-up auto delivery of gas or oil supply. * _____ _____
- Notify your gas or oil company to turn off supply. _____ _____
- Wood burning fireplaces not being used close flue and cap chimney.* _____ _____
- Remove and store grill, deck chairs and tables.* _____ _____
- Install insulated freeze protectors over outside faucets.* _____ _____
- Have a landscaper shut off and drain your sprinkler system.* _____ _____
- Clean carpet and upholstery, and wash and dry all bedding.* _____ _____
- Ensure all linens are clean, dry, and packed away. _____ _____
- Remove food from the refrigerator, clean, and install odor absorber. _____ _____
- Install odor absorber in closets to prevent musty smells.* _____ _____
- Unplug all electronics and appliances. _____ _____
- Close all window and door blinds.* _____ _____
- Turn off non-essential circuit breakers. _____ _____
- Install or activate hurricane shutters for storm and security protection. _____ _____
- Notify police department, and give them a contact number. _____ _____
- Arrange for a property management company or permanent resident to check on your property. _____ _____
- Stop newspaper delivery, and notify the post office to forward you mail. _____ _____
- Activate your alarm system.* _____ _____
- Install tape over exterior keyholes to prevent corrosion.* _____ _____

12

Hurricane Preparedness

W atch flags are posted to warn of the impending storm, high surf, and rip currents.

Millions of coastal residents are threatened by hurricanes each year. A lack of hurricane awareness and preparation can cause serious personal injury and property damage.

The goal of this chapter is to inform coastal homeowners about the potential damage of each hurricane category, review hurricane hazards, and provide tips that can be used to reduce damage to your home. Protecting the areas where severe winds, rain from torrential downpours, and flying debris can enter. Being informed and prepared is a responsibility all coastal home-owners share.

This Chapter Includes
Hurricane Preparedness
Hurricane Classifications
What Do You Do?
Stand-by Generators
Emergency Contact List

Ahurricane is not merely a bad storm, nor is it just strong winds with heavy rains. A hurricane is a serious, potentially life-and property-threatening event that should never be taken lightly. If you are in an area and there is a hurricane warning and evacuation announcement, evacuate! Too often, there is a name for people who choose to ride out the storm: *victims.*

Once you leave your home and get yourself and your family to safety, your concern will probably be, "Will my house still be there after the storm? What kind of damage will it have suffered?"

Always follow evacuation routes.

There are volumes written on hurricane preparedness—from pamphlets the Red Cross, emergency management, and other community organizations hand out, describing "go-bags" and emergency kits, to the detailed evacuation plans written by towns and cities. However, when we talk about hurricane preparedness here, we are talking about one thing: preparing your house to structurally survive a devastating storm.

We have already learned about roofs in an earlier chapter, emphasizing the need to have a roofing system that is rated for high winds. However, when it comes to protecting your home in a hurricane, your doors and windows are your points of greatest vulnerability. In chapter two, we discussed the importance of having doors and windows designed and rated for coastal areas. We introduced you to design pressure (DP) and impact zone (IZ) rated doors and windows to maximize protection from flying debris and wind-driven rain.

Storm clouds moving in can be a serious threat to life and property.

The Federal Emergency Management Agency (FEMA) defines a hurricane as "a type of tropical cyclone," the generic term for a low-pressure system that gradually forms in the tropics. A typical cyclone is accompanied by thunderstorms and, in the northern hemisphere, a counter-clockwise circulation of winds near the earth's surface.

All Atlantic and Gulf of Mexico coastal areas are subject to hurricanes or tropical storms. Parts of the southwestern United States and the pacific coast experience heavy rains and floods each year from hurricanes spawned off of Mexico's coast. The Atlantic hurricane season lasts from June to November, with the peak season being from mid-August to late October. Hurricanes can cause catastrophic damage to coastlines and several hundred miles inland. Winds can exceed 155 miles per hour.

Hurricanes and tropical storms can also spawn tornadoes and microburst's, create storm surges along the coast, and cause extensive damage from torrential rainfall.

HURRICANE CLASSIFICATIONS

Hurricanes are classified into five categories based on their wind speed, central pressure, and damage potential. Category three hurricanes and higher are considered major hurricanes, though categories one and two are still extremely dangerous and warrant your full attention.

- **A Hurricane Watch** means a hurricane is possible in your area. Be prepared to evacuate. Monitor local radio and television news or listen to NOAA weather radio for latest updates and developments.

- **A Hurricane Warning** is when a hurricane is expected in your area. If local authorities advise you to evacuate, leave immediately.

- **Category One: 74-95 miles per hour**
  Storm surge generally 4-5 feet above normal, minor damage to exterior of homes, and minor coastal flooding. Very dangerous winds will produce some damage.

- **Category Two: 96-110 miles per hour**
  Storm surge generally 6-8 feet above normal, major damage to exterior of homes. Extremely dangerous winds will cause extensive damage.

- **Category Three: 111-130 miles per hour**
  Storm surge generally 9-12 feet above normal, can cause flooding and some structural damage to buildings and mobile homes. Devastating damage will occur.

- **Category Four: 131-155 miles per hour**
  Storm surge generally 13-18 feet above normal can cause inland flooding, major beach erosion, and destruction to roof systems. Catastrophic damage will occur.

- **Category Five: 156 miles per hour and up**
  Storm surge generally greater than 18 feet above normal can cause catastrophic damage to all types of structures and buildings, can blow roofs off their structures, and can create major and severe coastal and inland flooding.

In short, hurricanes are nothing to trifle with. Driving winds and rain, however, are only part of the threat to your home. Those winds do more than simply bend trees; they uproot them. They lift just about anything not bolted down and toss it through the air like a paper glider. Once your roof is blown off, the walls will collapse, your possessions will blow away, and you will come back to nothing.

In other words, almost anything can become a flying missile capable of doing terrible damage to your home. If a tree becomes uprooted and falls on your house, or some huge object comes flying at your house, there is little you can do to save the house's structural integrity. But if smaller objects, such as lawn furniture, your neighbor's gardening tools, pieces of fence, or shingles, hit your house, there are things you can do.

What Do You Do?

Your primary goal in preparing your house to survive a hurricane is to keep the winds and rain from entering your house. Secure outside objects that might become debris. Garbage cans, garden tools, toys, signs, deck furniture, and a number of other harmless items become deadly missiles in hurricane winds. Water can do serious damage, but the wind (and the dynamics of the hurricane) will cause pressure changes inside your home, which can blow your roof off (even if it is a wind-rated roof).

If you are a do-it-yourselfer, that might mean covering your windows and doors with ½-inch or ⁵/8-inch exterior plywood or oriented strand board (OSB). You will need to nail or screw the plywood around the perimeter of each window and door opening.

The better, and more aesthetically pleasing, way to protect your house is to install shutters and shutter systems that can be instantly activated to protect your home. These protection systems are not expensive when compared to the value of your property. When weighed against the potential damage and destruction that can be caused by the hurricane, they are often a very wise investment. Reference the Coastal Products Directory.

Electric rolling shutter in the open position. The right photo shows two electric rolling shutters in the down position. This type of shutter is very effective at preventing flying debris from impacting the window. They are also good at preventing wind-driven rain from entering the house through a window or door seal. Rolling shutters provide excellent security protection.

 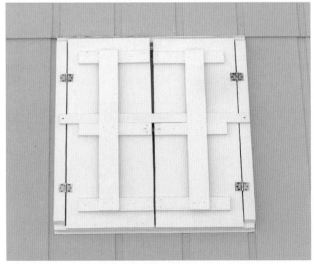

Barn-style storm shutter in the open position. The right photo shows a barn-style shutter in the closed position. This type of shutter can compliant a home and is very effective at keeping flying debris from impacting the window but not as effective at keeping out wind-driven rain. In the closed position there is a gap between the two panels and the hinges.

Corrugated panels come in clear polycarbonate and aluminum metal. They are very effective against flying debris but not so effective against wind-driven rain. Wind-driven rain from hurricane forced winds can sometimes blow-in behind the panels. A lesson learned...

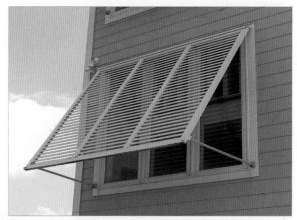

Bahama-style shutters have year round beauty. They come in many colors to compliment your home. They are very effective against flying debris; but not as effective against wind-driven rain. The individual louvers cannot be closed. The left photo shows a Bahama shutter in the closed position, and the right photo shows a Bahama shutter in the open position.

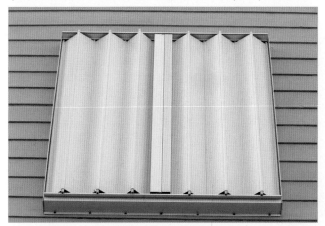

Accordion shutters in the closed position. The right photo shows accordion shutters in the open position. Accordion-style shutters are very effective against flying debris, wind-driven rain and intruders.

Stand-by Generators

A stand-by generator is a backup electrical system that operates automatically whether you are at home or away. Residential generators are fueled by natural gas or liquid propane gas. If you lose power, the generator will come on and supply electrical power to your house through your panel box. Coastal storms or hurricanes often cause power outages. In recent years, backup generators have increased in popularity in coastal areas. A generator will provide your everyday necessities, such as lights, appliances, heating, and cooling. Generators will automatically shut off when the power comes back on.

When choosing a home generator, look for a corrosion-resistant outer shell or cabinet, designed for the salt-air and coastal conditions. The outer shell of this generator is comprised of a dense and rugged composite material making it completely impervious to salt-air and salt-spray. Generators require periodic oil and filter changes to ensure lasting performance. (Photo courtesy of Kohler Company.) Reference the Coastal Products Directory.

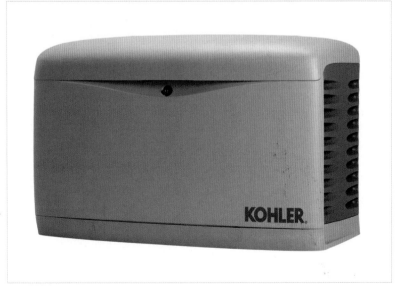

Emergency Contact Numbers

This is a list of contacts that you will need on hand in case of an emergency:

- Police Department_____

- Sheriff's Department_____

- State Highway Patrol_____

- Fire/Rescue Department_____

- Emergency Management—County _____

- Emergency Management—City_____

- FEMA—Federal Emergency Management_____

- City Hall or Town Hall_____

- Utility Company_____

- Gas Company_____

- Cable Company_____

- Roofing Contractor_____

- Electrical Contractor_____

- HVAC Contractor_____

- Water Restoration Specialist_____

- General Contractor_____

- **Note:** *For more information on hurricane preparedness go to www.ready.gov to prepare, plan and stay informed.*

13

Increasing Rental Income

Vacationers are always looking for a more relaxing and better vacation experience. Why not have a big beach umbrella available. Or have a beach-gear rental company deliver one on demand, so family and friends can relax in the shade.

Coastal homeowners will often list their property on the vacation rental market to the millions of vacationers traveling to the coastal shores each year. The one interest that each homeowner has in common is the desire to maximize their annual rental income. The coastal rental market is becoming more competitive. Owners can no longer rely on one or two features for a guaranteed income.

In this chapter you will discover how you can increase your vacation rental income with proven tips, techniques, and strategies—information that can also increase your property value; and help you maintain a competitive edge in today's coastal rental market.

This Chapter Includes
Maximizing Income
Guest Expectations
Amenities and Upgrades
Housekeeping
Living and Dining Areas
Kitchen and Laundry
Linens
Baths and Bedrooms
Built-ins

Coastal homes for many of you may be your primary residence or second home, while others will purchase or build a home for investment purposes. After all, the very same reasons that attract people to live in a coastal area are the reasons millions of vacationers travel to the coast and book a rental property. Have you ever thought about what draws people to the coastal areas? Maybe it is the smell of the salt air or the warm ocean breeze or just walking on the beach and watching a family of dolphins in the surf. It is a place where memories are made with your family and friends.

Maximizing Income

Everything we have discussed regarding your home is valid, regardless of whether it is your primary residence, second home, or investment property or whether you are just thinking about moving to the coast. However, there are other things you can do to maximize the return on your investment.

How about local restaurants? Provide information on different dining experiences from pizza parlors to fine dining establishments; include descriptions and phone numbers, and don't forget to include local shops and grocery stores.

There is a great demand for homes that are handicap-accessible with wheelchair ramps and elevators. When your guests have children, does your house provide appropriate safety features?

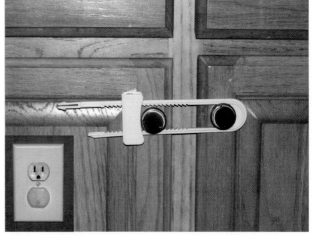

A child-safety gate that can be set up for children or pets.

Main photo: Child-safety latch.
Insert photo: receptacle with safety plug.

Pricing your vacation home is one of the most important decisions you will make. A property management company's goal is to ensure your property's weekly, monthly, or annual rental rates are competitive. This will help increase bookings for your home. The rental management company will advertise your property on the internet and in print; most bookings are made through the internet. The rental agency is compensated by charging a percentage of the rental income. Additional charges may include housekeeping, linens, repairs, and pool and hot tub maintenance. The more annual income, the more you can offset expenses.

Vacationers are always looking for a better vacation experience. That experience starts with the accommodations. When decorating, you should bring the relaxed atmosphere of the beach into your house. Use a casual beach theme to decorate and personalize a room. Bring in elements from the beach, such as seashells, driftwood, coral, and nets.

Find a location to hang a hammock, so your guests can lie back and relax in the ocean breeze.

Destination weddings are very popular, and the beach offers a beautiful natural and romantic atmosphere. With the summer breeze and the sound of the surf, beach weddings are very special. Ask your rental agency to include your property as a location for weddings and special events.

If your guests are looking for a more active vacation, ask your rental agency if they can provide a welcome packet with information on local golf, tennis, fishing, museums, historic sites, aquariums, water sports, kayaking, and other local events.

Surf fishing is enjoyable and relaxing for many vacationers.

Summertime water sports are fun for the entire family.

Guest Expectations

The expectations of today's guests are very high. It is important to update your property in style and modern conveniences. A drop in repeat guests is one of the first signs that they are shopping elsewhere. This could be due to the condition of the property, or the rental rates may need to be more competitive. Be careful when increasing your rental rates. Just one week not rented may cost you more than a modest increase will make you during the entire rental season. Be prepared. Depending on the economy, guests may want to negotiate a modest discount. If you have made recent improvements to your property, notify your rental agency, so they can update new photos for the Internet or brochures.

Amenities and Upgrades

To achieve a more desirable rate for your home, here is a list of amenities and upgrades to consider: hot tubs and swimming pools, free long-distance calling, cordless phones with answering machines, high-speed wireless Internet, flat-screen cable TVs with premium channels, DVD/CD players with DVDs and CDs, books, puzzles, board games, bicycles, a grill, beach chairs, an iron and ironing boards, hair dryers in every bath, soap, shampoo, and conditioner in every bath, a well-stocked laundry center, and a well-equipped kitchen. If it is something that would make your own stay more inviting, have it available for your guests.

A swimming pool. This is always a desirable amenity for your guests.

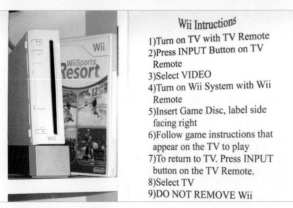

Interactive gaming will provide entertainment for everyone on those rainy days at the beach. **Note**: *Always include detailed instructions for your guest.*

It may not be the chocolate on the pillow, but few things say "welcome" like a gift basket.

135

Housekeeping

Amenities and upgrades like hot tubs are important. However, to ensure repeat rentals, housekeeping is the number-one priority for guest satisfaction. Detailing and verifying that a property has been thoroughly cleaned after each guest departs is very important.

Housekeeping and cleaning issues may include the following: identifying repairs, putting furniture back in the proper location, inspecting and cleaning carpet and upholstery, cleaning area rugs and bedding as required, cleaning hot tubs and pools, and maintaining property grounds, along with a thorough cleaning of the entire home.

Always have someone evaluate the need for carpet and upholstery cleaning between rentals.

The following photos show additional upgrades and amenities that will maximize your rental income and keep your property at a competitive advantage.

Of course, the most important thing you are renting is the house itself. You want it to be welcoming, comfortable, and beautiful.

Beautiful coastal sunsets draw vacationers from far away.

Guests love bicycles, even if they don't ride them! Just having them available encourages their desire for long bike rides by the beach.

Make sure your bicycles are clean, rust free, and kept inside when not in use. Most bicycles are made of metal that will rust and corrode very quickly in the coastal environment.

A bicycle not made for the coastal environment. The chain, sprocket, frame, and rims are severely corroded.

Photo of a Hampton Cruiser. Reference the Coastal Products Directory for a list of bicycles designed for the coastal environment.

Bicycles built for the coastal environment will have (at a minimum), aluminum frame, stainless steel spokes, and alloy rims with a chain and sprocket that is corrosion resistant.

Depending on your property, you may want to consider such high-end amenities as a putting green. Have extra golf clubs and golf balls available for your guests to use. Have a croquet set available to set up for lawn croquet.

People on vacation like to grill out. Providing a clean and functional grill is a major addition for your guests. Make sure your rental agency is aware you have a gas grill so they can make arrangements to have the propane tanks exchanged as needed.

Grills and beach chairs are favorite amenities for your guest. Beach umbrellas, water boards, kites, and floats are other great amenities that guest can use to make their stay more enjoyable. **Note:** *Always keep a grill cover over your grill when not in use. If possible, place it in a storage room for maximum protection from the salt-air environment.*

Unlike inland areas, the coast can be tough on grills. There are stainless steel grills that will corrode very quickly in a coastal environment, as the **middle photo** shows—especially the closer you are to the coast. Both middle and bottom photos are examples of low-grade stainless steel grills. As we have already discussed in chapter one, there are different grades of stainless, and some are more corrosive-resistant than others. How can you tell? A simple magnet test, as shown in the **bottom photo**, can give a coastal homeowner valuable information before making a purchase. Replacing rusty grills can get expensive.

If a magnet sticks to a stainless steel grill, the grill will probably be made of a ferritic grade, 400 series stainless steel. The grill will corrode and bleed rust as shown in the **middle photo**. It will be cheaper because it contains very little nickel, the primary metal that makes stainless steel non-magnetic. If a magnet doesn't stick to a stainless grill, it will probably be made of an austenitic grade, 300 series type 304 or 316 stainless steel, a higher-grade stainless containing more nickel and chromium. Type 316 marine grade stainless steel grills are highly corrosive resistant, with a higher percentage of nickel and chromium than 304 stainless steel. They are also very limited and more expensive. The corroded grill and the new grill with the magnet are not made of type 304 or 316 stainless. Type 304 stainless steel grills may form a light surface pitting

A small magnet can save you time, money, and frustration.

the closer you live to the coast—particularly on oceanfront properties, piers, and docks. Type 304 is very corrosive resistant; it is not as expensive as 316 stainless steel and will last for years in coastal environment, but it's not corrosion proof. **Note:** *Use a commercial rust remover, like Naval Jelly, to remove light surface corrosion. Reference the Coastal Products Directory for stainless steel grills.*

Living Area

A living room with a flat-screen cable TV with a DVD player and DVDs is a very attractive amenity. Most living areas have direct access to a main deck. The main deck is great for entertaining or just enjoying the view.

Keeping your carpet cleaned after your guest departs can get expensive. The high maintenance carpet has been replaced by a laminate floor. *Note: Before installing laminate or hardwood flooring in your coastal home, make sure your windows and doors seals are designed to keep out wind-driven rain from coastal storms.*

A wet bar with an additional ice maker and sink for making those cool summertime beverages. Also, the cabinets are great for storing games, DVDs, and books for your guests to enjoy.

Dining Area

Your guests are most likely not looking to have large, formal meals. They are probably looking for enjoyable, informal meals. With that in mind, make sure your dining area is large enough to accommodate all the guests who might be staying in the house, and make sure you have enough flatware and place settings on hand for everyone. Keep your dining area neat, uncluttered, and filled with light.

If you can fulfill these needs and make your guests feel welcomed and comfortable while your rates remain competitive, you will have a very successful rental property.

Dining chairs with machine-washable slipcovers that can be washed between rentals.

Dining chairs without slipcovers are high maintenance, requiring frequent cleaning to remove stains. Some stains may be impossible to remove. The chairs will need to be upholstered every few years.

Kitchens and Laundry

Kitchens should be neat, uncluttered, well equipped, and well organized. If there is an appliance that you feel needs clear instructions, laminate the instructions, and leave them in an easily accessible area. The same is true for a washer and dryer, they have become more advanced. Washers and dryers now have information or default codes that display when there is a problem. Solutions to these default codes are in your owners manual. Have your owner's manual accessible or laminate these default codes and place them where your guest can see them. It maybe a problem your guest can easily resolve, saving them time while on vacation, and saving you a costly service call. Example: Default code "dc", normally means unbalance load preventing your washer from spinning. All your guest will need to do, is redistribute the load. There are other default codes that are just as simple to resolve.

Linens

Towels, bedding, and pillows are a must. Beds should be made when your guests arrive. Towels should be folded. Linen closets should have extra blankets. Make sure your linen closets are neat and organized, and extra hangers are always appreciated.

An iron and ironing board, extra clothes hangers, and a laundry basket on each floor with bedrooms are extra amenities that make your guests feel at home. Fabric refresher and wrinkle-release products for clothes are extra perks.

Baths

Bathrooms should be cleaned and restocked with bath linens and bath tissue. For an added treat, provide a hairdryer and shampoo/soap dispensers in all baths.

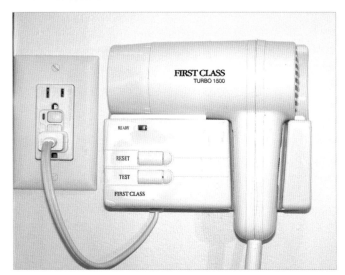

Bedrooms

Bedrooms should be clean, roomy, and airy. They should never be cluttered. Make sure your bedrooms are attractive and inviting, and your guests will return for many more years. It is also a good idea to have a TV in all the bedrooms. Upgrade to flat-screen, cable TVs with DVD players. **Note:** *To remove spots and stains quickly between rentals (the time allotted between a guest check-out and guest check-in), comforters, quilts, and coverlets should be machine washable.*

▊ Built-ins

Built-ins are a great use of space. They are usually designed to maximize the area they are built into. The bottom left photo shows a convenient mini bar installed in the furniture cabinet of the master suite.

A corner space before the built-in fireplace and TV were added.

After the built-in was added. The electric fire-place and flat-screen TV add value, while utilizing the corner space in the most efficient way.

The built-in to the right was created by filling in a recessed corner, as shown in the left photo. Inside the cabinet is a set of drawers and an area for gaming accessories. The flat-screen TV is now mounted in the cabinet.

Have you ever noticed; when you stay in a hotel or resort; how close beverages and snacks are to your room, if not already in a mini-bar in the room? Coastal homes are often multi-level, and not all conveniences are readily accessible to your guests if they want a midnight snack. Surprise your guests with built-in areas that make their stay more welcoming and convenient. With prior planning, built-ins are not that difficult or expensive to install. They add value for your guests and with that comes increased rental income. This refreshment center was created out of empty wall space several years after the home was built.

Mark and Patti's dream had become something of a nightmare. However, to their credit they were determined to enjoy their beach house.

"We knew this was where we wanted to be," Patti said.
"We just made some mistakes," Mark noted, shaking his head in mild disgust. "I wish I had known then what I know now."

As the first winter and summer and then the next winter passed, Mark and Patti learned that some of their choices were ill-suited to the coastal environment and that they had no choice but to "bite the bullet" and redo their mistakes. The two costliest "fixes" were replacing the siding and putting in a air-conditioning unit.

"We were lucky—which is a lot different than being knowledgeable," Mark acknowledged. "Replacing the siding and the air conditioner was painful, but at least I knew that the replacements were done correctly—and with materials well-suited to our house and where we live."
Local zoning codes had guaranteed that the windows that had been installed during their construction met the demands of the environment—saving them another potential nightmare cost.

With the major work of re-siding and replacing their AC unit behind them, Mark and Patti went about taking care of the smaller "hassle" issues that had come up.

"Every weekend was another project," Mark said. "Replacing hinges and hardware, repainting, whatever." He shrugged. "But what are you going to do? Every house is a project."

Patti smiled. "We've been in the house three years now. It wasn't as easy as we wanted or expected, but it is our house and we love being here."

"Sometimes I still hit myself for how stupid I was," Mark confessed with a rueful smile. "I mean, we thought we'd done our research. We visited this place a hundred time, but we were just so caught up in where it was that we didn't look closely enough at the details. And when it comes to a house, especially one in a coastal area, details matter. Right down to the nails and screws you use."

After three years, the "sting" of going back and redoing their original work has eased. The house is everything they wanted it to be. The garden is in bloom. It is, as Patti proclaimed, "perfect."

Mark and Patti's dream house went from being a dream house to being a nightmare to being a dream house again. When you are looking for your dream house, take advantage of the information in this book. **Do it right the first time.**

Mark and Patti are happy in their house. But, without hesitation, they would be the first to tell you that they would rather have done it right from the beginning.

Mark and Patti can now enjoy those beautiful sunsets, knowing that their coastal cottage is once again their dream home.

APPENDIX—Coastal Products Directory

Coastal homeowners are not always familiar with the many new products designed and manufactured for coastal regions, such as products that are resistant to high winds, salt-air, corrosion, wind-driven rain, and products that are impact resistant. The following companies manufacture and market their products to coastal homeowners. To expedite your online search, for coastal products you may enter the following key words: coastal, salt-air, wind-driven rain, stainless steel, wind-rated, impact resistant, noncorrosive, and corrosion resist.

Chapter One
Hardware, Fasteners, and Nails

National
www.natman.com
Hinges and latches
1-800-346-9445

Stanley Bostitch
www.bostitch.com
Fasteners and nails
1-800-556-6696

Simpson StrongTie
www.strongtie.com
Fasteners and nails
1-800-999-5099

Tie Down Engineering
www.tiedown.com
Marine hardware
1-404-344-0000

Corbin Russwin
www.corbinrusswin.com
Stainless Steel entry hardware
1-800-543-3658

Schlage
www.schlage.com
Solid brass entry hardware
1-888-805-9833

Baldwin Hardware Corp.
www.baldwinhardware.com
Solid brass entry hardware
1-800-566-1986

Chapter Two
Doors and Windows

PGT Industries
www.pgtindustries.com
DP50 windows/impact patio doors
1-800-282-6019

Jamsill Guard
www.jamsill.com
Sill pans
1-800-526-7455

Weathershield Windows and Doors
www.weathershield.com
Lifeguard line
1-800-222-2995

Pactiv Building Products
www.greenguard.pactiv.com
Building wrap
1-800-241-4402

Anderson Windows and Doors
www.andersonwindows.doors.com
Storm watch protection
1-800-426-4261

Marvin Windows and Doors
www.marvin.com
Storm plus protection
1-888-537-7828

Pella Windows and Doors
www.pella.com
Hurricane shield protection
1-888-288-7281

Jeld-Wen Windows and Doors
www.jeld-wen.com
Impact gard protection
1-800-535-3936

Simonton Windows and Doors
www.simonton.com
Storm breaker plus
1-800-746-6686

Atrium Windows and Door
www.atrium.com
Safe Harbor windows and doors
1-800-969-6866

Therma-Tru Doors
www.thermatru.com
Tru-Defense door system
1-800-843-7628

Gorell Window and Doors
www.gorell.com
Hurricane impact doors and windows
1-800-946-7355

Overhead Door Company
www.overheaddoor.com
Garage doors
1-800-929-1277

Harmann Doors
www.harmann.us
Garage doors
1-877-654-6762

LARSON
www.larsondoors.com
Storm doors
1-800-352-3360

Chapter Three
Exterior Siding and Trim

CertainTeed
www.certainteed.com
Siding and trim
1-800-782-8777

Versatex
www.Versatex.com
PVC trim products
724-857-1111

Plycem Trim
www.plycemtrim.com
Fiber-cement trim
1-877-467-5923

Azek Building Products
www.azek.com
PVC trim products
1-877-275-2935

Dow Weathermate Wind-Lock
www.wind-lock.com
House wrap
1-800-872-5625

The Foundry
www.foundrysiding.com
Siding and trim
1-800-771-4486

Royal Group
www.royalbuildingproducts.com
Siding and trim
1-800-387-2789

Chapter Four
Coastal Heating and Cooling

Amana Heating and Cooling
www.amana-hac.com
Salt spray tested
1-877-254-4729

Trane Heating
www.trane.com
Weather Guard™
1-903-581-3200

Maytag Heating and Cooling
www.maytaghvac.com
Salt spray tested
1-866-262-9824

Carrier Heating and Cooling
www.residential.carrier.com
Weather Aroma™
1-800-227-7437

Goodman Heating and Cooling
www.goodmanmfg.com
Salt spray tested
1-877-254-4729

Nutone Heating and Cooling
www.nutonehvac.com
Salt spray tested
1-800-422-4328

Chapter Five
Exterior Electrical Components

Murray Meter Products
www.sea.siemans.com
Murray convert/products/metering
Meter-Base Enclosures
1-800-241-4453

Milbank Manufacturing
www.milbankmfg.com
Meter-base enclosures
1-877-483-5314

Wave Lighting
www.wavelighting.com
Exterior lighting
1-877-870-9283

Seagull Lighting
www.seagulllighting.com
Exterior lighting
1-800-347-5483

Incon Lighting
www.inconlighting.com
Exterior lighting
1-800-393-5630

Chapter Six
Coastal Decks

Azek
www.azek.com
Cellular PVC decking
1-877-275-2935

Trex
www.trex.com
Composite decking
1-800-289-8739

Timbertech
www.timbertech.com
Composite decking
1-800-307-7780

Gossen Decking Products
www.gossencorp.com
Cellular PVC decking
1-800-558-8984

AridDeck
www.wahoodecks.com
Aluminum decking
1-877-270-9387

Correct Building Products LLC
www.correctdeck.com
Composite decking
1-877-332-5877

Strongrail/Strongdek
www.strongwell.com
Fiberglass decking and handrail
1-276-645-8000

Underdeck
www.underdeck.com
Under-deck drainage
1-877-805-7156

Engineered Plastic System
www.epsplascticlumber.com
Engineered plastic decking
1-800-480-2327

American Dry Deck
www.americandrydeck.com
Under-deck drainage
1-888-416-7668

FSI Home Products
www.locdry.com
Aluminum decking
1-888-739-6172

Dek Drain
www.dekdrain.com
Under-deck drainage
1-866-335-3724

Tamko (Decks/Roofing)
www.tamko.com
Composite and PVC decking
1-800-641-4691

W.R Grace and Company
www.grace.com
Vycor deck products
1-800-354-5414

Corts Clean
www.corteclean.com
Deck cleaner
1-800-203-2202

Solair Awning
www.solair.com
Deck awning
1-866-888-8120

Rolling Shield Awning
www.rollingsheild.com
Deck awning
1-800-474-9404

Sunsetter Awning
www.sunsetter.com
Deck awning
1-800-876-2340

Sunesta Products
www.sunesta.com.
Deck awning
1-800-874-2001

Poly~Wood
www.polywoodinc.com
Out door furniture
1-877-457-3284

Chapter Seven
Exterior Surface Preparation

Star-brite (Rust Eater)
www.starbrite.com
Rust remover
1-800-327-8583

Loctite
www.loctiteproducts.com
Rust treatment
1-800-624-7767

Ace Hardware and Paint
www.acehardware.com
Paint and Finishes
1-866-290-5334

Sherwin Williams
www.sherwinwilliams.com
Paint and finishes
1-800-474-3794

Valspar Paint
www.valsparpaint.com
Paint and finishes
1-800-845-9061

Olympic Paint
www.olympic.com
Paint and finishes
1-800-441-9695

Behr Paint
www.behr.com
Paint and finishes
1-800-854-0133

True Value Hardware
www.truevalue.com
Paint and finishes
1-877-502-4641

Benjamin Moore Paints
www.bengaminmoore.com
Paint and finishes
1-888-236-6667

Glidden Paint
www.glidden.com
Paint and finishes
1-800-454-3336

Minwax
www.minwax.com
Wood stains and finishes
1-800-523-9299

Cabot
www.cabotstain.com
Wood stains and sealers
1-800-878-8246

Thompson Water Seal
www.thompsonwaterseal.com
Wood sealer/preservatives
1-800-367-6297

Chapter Eight
Water Heaters

Rheems
www.rheems.com
Marathon series
1-800-621-5622

A.O. Smith
www.aosmith.co
DynaClean™
1-866-362-9898

Whirlpool Water Heaters
www.whirlpoolwaterheaters.com
Stainless steel heating elements
1-877-817-6750

Culligan
www.culligan.com
Water softeners
1-877-487-3695

Kinetico Water Systems
www.kinetico.com
Water softeners
1-800-944-9283

Chapter Nine
Coastal Roofing

CertainTeed Roofing
www.certinteed.com
Hatteras Shingles
1-800-345-1145

Metals USA Roofing (Gerard Roofs)
www.metalsusaroofing.com
Stone-coated metal roof
1-866-919-7663

Owens Corning
www.owenscorning.com
Weather guard/duration shingles
1-800-438-7465

Peterson Aluminum
www.pac-clad.com
Aluminum standing seam roofs
1-800-272-4482

Follansbee Metal Roofs
www.follansbeeroofing.com
Stainless steel standing seam roofs
1-800-624-6906

GAF Material Corporation
www.gaf.com
Grand Slate and Grand Canyon shingles
1-877-423-7663

EDCO Products
www.edcoproducts.com
Metal slate and shake shingles
1-800-333-2580

Tamko Building Products
www.tamko.com
Heritage Shingles
1-800-641-4691

Chapter Ten
Preventive Maintenance

Luxury Metals
www.luxurymetals.com
Vent caps
1-206-406-7346

Simpson Dura-Vent
www.duravent.com
Vent caps
1-800-835-4429

Artis Metals Company
www.artiscaps.com
Vent caps
1-800-892-2277

Chapter Eleven
Winterizing Coastal Homes

Star-brite Antifreeze
www.starbrite.com
Nontoxic antifreeze
1-800-327-8583

Camco Antifreeze
www.shipsstore.com
Nontoxic antifreeze
1-877-744-7786

Chapter Twelve
Hurricane Preparedness

Kohler Company
www.kohlerpower.com
Residential generators
1-800-544-2444

Generac
www.generac.com
Residential generators
1-888-436-372

Cummins Onan
www.cumminsonan.com
Residential generators
1-800-888-6626

Alutech United
www.alutech.com
Storm/security protection
1-800-233-1144

Croci North America
www.crocinorthamerica.com
Storm/security protection
1-800-951-1195

QMI Corporation
www.qmiusa.com
Storm/security protection
1-866-980-1750

Folding Shutter Corporation
www.foldingshutter.com
Storm/security protection
1-800-643-6371

Atlantic Premium Shutters
www.atlanticpremiumshutters.com
Storm/security protection
1-866-288-2726

Chapter Thirteen
Increasing Rental Income

Hampton Bicycles
www.hamptoncruisers.com
Cruisers
1-800-222-0570

Schwinn Bicycles
www.schwinn.com
Cruisers
1-800-626-2811

Sun Bicycles
www.sunbicycles.com
Cruisers
1-305-238-1866

Trex Bicycles
www.trekbikes.com
Cruisers
1-800-879-8735

Jamis Bicycles
www.jamisbike.com
Cruisers
1-800-222-0570

Wilmington Grill Company
www.wilmingtongrill.com
Stainless steel grills
1-910-793-1345

Coastal Gas grills
www.coastalgasgrills.com
Stainless steel grills
1-918-660-4989

Holland Grill Company
www.hollandgrill.com
Stainless steel grills
1-919-557-2001

Phoenix grill Company
www.newphoenixgrills.com
Stainless steel grills
1-888-781-4657

Solair Infrared Grills
www.rasmussen.biz/grills
Stainless steel grills
1-562-698-8718

MAGMA Products (Grills)
www.magmaproducts.com
Stainless steel grills
1-562-627-0500

Addresses /Phone Numbers

Name and Address	**Phone**